HOW TO BE A Young Lady

2ND EDITION

YOUR TOTAL GUIDE FOR BEING THE BEST POSSIBLE YOU!

DARLENE AIKEN

Foreword by Kym Hampton, WNBA Legend

This book belongs to:

_____

Name

My favorite picture of
Me

Paste here

Contributors

Kym Hampton, Retired WNBA Legend, Spokeswoman for the NBA, WNBA, New York Liberty and New York Knicks, Actress, and Model

Ms. Hampton completed a 15 year professional basketball career not only in the WNBA, but Spain, Italy, France and Japan. The transition is natural because the world for Kym has always been a stage. A graduate of Arizona State University, she received her bachelor's degree in theater but will go down in the university's history books as one of the most decorated hoop players to wear a Sun Devil's jersey.

She has become a plus sized model in fashion as well as cosmetics. She is an original Cover Girl Queen Collection Model featured in a nation-wide commercial. She has found herself in GLAMOUR, ESSENCE and other magazines. The multi-talented Hampton has also had the opportunity to grace the television and film world during guest appearances on the "Cosby Show", "Rosie", NBA TV, Celebrity Wheel of Fortune, JuWanna Mann, to name a few.

Singing has always been a love of Kym's, and she was a regular at a nightclub (Insomnia) in Italy. Even before setting foot in Madison Square Garden as a player with the Liberty, Kym before a sell-out crowd-performed the national anthem during a Knicks play-off game. Since then, she has performed the anthem several times at the Garden and is currently working with the New York Liberty as a Fan Development Leader while pursuing other dreams.

Carlton Spence, Celebrity Fashion Stylist, Image Consultant, and Founder of Style Evolution, LLC

Carlton Spence has a keen and meticulous eye for fashion and style. As a result, his superb taste has drawn his repertoire of celebrities such as Bishop Hezekiah Walker, female race car driver, model and advertising spokeswoman, Danica Patrick, Gospel legend Shirley Caesar, JJ Hairston, Marvin Sapp, the cast of Nickelodeon, Coko Clemons of SWV, R. Kelly, Kelly Price, Chris Rock, Byron Cage, Deitrick Haddon, Avant, the Miss Black Collegiate USA Scholarship Pageant ™, InStyle Magazine, Naturalizer, Nina Shoes, Seventeen Magazine, Macy's, Nordstrom, Jones New York, and others.

Dr. Teresa Taylor, Psychologist & Founder, CEO and Publisher of TTW Associates Inc. /New York Trend

She has been an entrepreneur since the age of 22, she obtained a Master's in Psychology from the City University of New York, Queens College; a Master's in Management from Columbia University; and a Doctorate in Administration from Columbia University — all before the age of 30. She also holds a Master's in Clinical Counseling from Long Island University and is a member of the American Counselor's Association and the Independent Press.

Tiffany "The Budgetnista" Aliche, Financial Expert & Best-Selling Author of The One Week Budget

Tiffany is also a speaker and passionate teacher of fun, financial empowerment. Her company, "The Budgetnista", specializes in the delivery of financial literacy education. Tiffany has been a featured speaker at American Express, Princeton University, Columbia University, The New York Public Library, and The United Way as well as others. She and her financial advice have been featured in ESSENCE Magazine, FORBES, Fox Business, Black Enterprise, VIBE.com, as well as numerous online publications. She also blogs for The Huffington Post. Learn more at: http://thebudgetnista.biz/

Acknowledgements

First and foremost, I'd like to in the biggest way that I know how, which is still never big enough, say, "THANK YOU!!!" To my Lord and Savior, Jesus the Christ! The one who totally knows me better than I know myself. He never misconstrues my intentions, has total faith in me, made me in His image, and trusts that I am filled with greatness. Words cannot express how thankful I am that He found me. I never found Him because it was I who was lost NOT HIM!

I also thank God for selecting my family & parents, for it is with all that they are that I exist. I thank them for their consistent love and sacrifices for me – they're now my babies. A special shout out to my dad who is my rock! Love that man to pieces for his insight, his solicited and unsolicited advice and wisdom. Who always listens to what I have to say, even when he does not want to.

To my son who just by his existence gives me renewed hope, even when I wanted to give up. For his words of encouragement, his belief in me, and by his actions that prove he really HAS been listening to what I say.

To all those who support me and my projects, thank you! Kym Hampton who always supports my self-esteem endeavors for girls, who places support calls to my son in college to encourage him, our countless conversations about many topics that we as women deal with, Carlton Spence, our multitude of conversations and church/preaching/testimonial sessions via phone, Renee Joshua-Porter and Wanda Mabray-Beckwith, our strong Sistahgurl conversations, inspiring moments, and tough love sessions, Tania and Ajamu Khalfani, my people! Nuff Said! My CI/ATL Crew that ALWAYS holds it down for me – Sonji, Patricia, Jenny, Renee, Rob, Shug, WC, Amp Hamp, Rev. Trey Trey, & Bishop Rosemary Lands. I thank you all from the bottom of my heart for believing in me and standing in my corner, even when standing in my corner has not always been easy. Thanks to Vanessa Edwards-El for being you and all that you do!

Special "thank you" to my editor, Miss Milani Porter, you were born great, you're becoming greater by the second, and your greatest is yet to come. Watch out world!

Thank you to Ni'cola Mitchell.....you ROCK!!!

To anyone who has ever sent words of encouragement and prayers, to those who wanted to, but didn't, to those who tried to deter

the dream, I say, "thank you!" God is
AWESOME!!!

Table of Contents

Foreword

When I was asked to write the Foreword for this book I felt a little scared. I also felt honored and knew this was something meant for me to do. I am honored because I, like Darlene, see empowering girls/women as a calling, as something necessary for the future state of humanity. I always say that, "if we as adults don't do everything we can to help mold our youth into confident well-rounded individuals, we are going to be some miserable old folk."

As I read through the pages I often felt Darlene and I were one. I, too, was that extremely tall thick girl that got picked on because of my size. I didn't take the bully route because I always had a soft spot for the underdog. When I got to high school, I talked my peers out of fighting, stealing or bullying lunch money (among other things) out of those poor souls. It was the first day of my freshman year of high school when the basketball coach saw me walking down the hall. He stopped me and asked if I would try out for the basketball team. At 6'0 tall, I was not trying to do anything that would bring attention to myself and/or make me look goofier than I already felt – but I thank God for that man's persistence, because he asked me every day until I said, "yes". I know God had something to do with me saying yes because when I said, "yes" there was a peace in my soul and I didn't look back.

I truly believe God sends intervention/angels to sometimes change the course of our lives. This is a blessing because rarely (especially when we are younger) do we see the gifts of greatness that each one of us has been blessed with.

While reading this book, I realized that not only will it give our young ladies the tools to accept and love who they are right now, but it will coach them on self-improvement. It guides them on what to expect of themselves and others, how to plan, how to get up when they fall, how to communicate their needs and issues, how to focus and set goals, how to function in any setting, but most importantly…how to look at themselves as whole and perfect just as God created them.

I know this guide is meant for young girls, but the reality is, many of us (older girls) didn't have that secure, confident, determined female figure to guide us along the way. Some of us have been incredibly blessed to accomplish a lot in life, but we often relax in those places, afraid to move on and do the other great stuff we are here to do. Why? We would exit our comfort zones. There are so many things I want to do, yet I remain stagnant, all the while rationalizing, to myself and others, why I can't or don't move forward.

This is a great workbook to have in any household. It is a great book to give as a gift. Not everything will work for everyone, but the guidelines are in place so you can reference and tweak it to fit you.

There are so many questions in this workbook that I have not asked myself in years, let alone have an answer to. I am grateful I had the chance to meet Darlene, for she is truly another angel sent to get me back on the course of making a difference, in not only my life, but the world.

May God bless you as you read this book, so you will always know WHO'S you are and that the love God has for **YOU** is like no other. Yes, you are the apple of God's eye!!!

Kym Hampton
WNBA Legend

Preface

My mother often tells the story about how I would get in the window as a little girl and yell that I wanted to go to school. She had to place me in pre-school, to quell the noise, and I've been in a learning institution (traditional and non-traditional) ever since. Given that I have always been interested in learning as much as I can, I use what I have learned to help others. As a result, I have managed to assist young girls, tweens, teens (boys and girls), and professional women become open to exploring new possibilities of how they see themselves, improve their self-esteem, and personal growth techniques.

I have earned the title, self-esteem expert, not solely because of my acquired knowledge in traditional educational settings, but from the "school of hard knocks". I remember growing up not liking anything about myself. I wanted to change my name, birthdate, hair, weight, and shoe size. I never wanted to change my sex, parents, siblings, or anything externally, just certain features that I thought would make me look and feel better. We have this natural propensity to seek approval to "fit in". I teach the students in my personal growth and freshman seminar courses about a renowned psychologist by the name of Abraham Maslow. Maslow introduced his theory of Human Motivation which, simply put, is that we, as humans are motivated by basic survival needs and we will do anything it takes to have these needs met. Within the hierarchy, there is loving/belongingness needs – they include friendship, family, affections, relationships, belonging in work and groups. However, I am of the notion, that this sense to want to belong first occurred back in the day of Adam and Eve when satan first told Eve that she surely would not die if she ate from the forbidden tree, but God just didn't want her to become like…this was to give her the impression that she needed to be someone other than herself, which also implies that her current existence was less than what should have been – not good enough (thanks Pastor) – you get the point! Fast forward to television, magazines, and other subliminal messages from external sources, no wonder it is imperative that our self-esteem is intact from the very beginning.

While growing up the television shows that I watched, my interaction with school teachers, and the magazine images had permeated my spirit and told me that I was not beautiful. My parents told me that I was, but the value was not placed on what my parents said, it was on what I saw and interacted with outside of their words, for those images and words seemed to have had louder voices. While change is what I sought, what was peculiar is I never thought to seek replacements. For example, I thought I didn't like my name, but I had not thought of another name that would be better. In fact, it was not until I realized that my father named me that I began to love my name because....well, next to the words "daddy's little girl" in the dictionary is my picture. The start of something great....but I would come to know that years later....many years later.

It was not until I was in the fifth grade that I had an epiphany. I did not know I had until much later when I reflected upon the pivotal points in my life that changed it forever, unbeknownst to me, at the time. I used to enjoy sitting next to a little girl on the bus named, Tanya. I thought she was everything that I was not – pretty. One day, Tanya did not get on the bus and one day turned into two days and two days turned into the remainder of the week, which in the mind of a fifth grader, is an eternity. Once Tanya returned, I began to inquire about her absences. She shared with me that she was in foster care because her parents were both killed in a car accident and she and her siblings lived in separate homes. While I was not certain about what, exactly foster care was, the siblings living in separate homes did not "sit" right with me. She further explained that the week she was out was the only week all of the foster mothers could coincide their schedules so that all siblings could visit one another. I remember how it was as if all of my insides sunk in, to the point of feeling hollow. It was at that moment that something inside of me

4

felt that as pretty as I thought Tanya was, I would not trade being pretty for giving up my family and my life as I knew it.

In my mind, I remember thinking that, while my siblings would get on my nerve and "make me sick!" I never wanted to have to make an appointment to fight with, annoy, watch cartoons, run the risk of getting in trouble for being unable to stop laughing at the dinner table when our parents said to be quiet, or any of the times we shared that were good or not so good. I also realized, at that point, that I took for granted that I had both my mother and father and extended family. While I failed miserably, on countless occasions, at the promise I made to myself that I would never ever ever get mad at my parents, again, nor declare major hatred for them when I could not get my way, it did change how I felt about them and made me appreciate them more.

Some years down the road, I had another epiphany. This is the time when I realized, still reflecting on Tanya, that I could change my weight, my attitude, how I felt about me and others, but there are some things that I cannot change and that is because, I'm not supposed to. What I'm supposed to do is spend my time changing what I can change and once I do that, I will find that I've spent an enormous amount of time on one issue, alone.

This was especially true for me because at a very young age I was taller than everyone, including the teacher. I was also overweight and because the first letter of my last name starts with A, I had to sit in the first seat in the first row. This meant that I was subjected to many many fat jokes and insults. I was, in my mind, having to decide to either go through my entire day feeling sad and having no friends or using my height and weight to my advantage and become a bully. I opted for the latter. As a result, people ceased the jokes, at least to my face, and I was able to play with whomever I chose because they were afraid to not let me play.

In this age where bullying seems to be a new phenomenon, it really is not. Bullying, while I was growing up was just as "real" then as it is today, and in some cases more harmful. I realize that cyber bullying is a different concept, however, its core is derived from lacking the same thing….low self-esteem. Also, adults and others are extremely harsh on those who are bullies and sympathetic for the victims of the bully. I say, that both the bully and the bullied are both suffering from low self-esteem, but each has chosen to deal with it from a different point.

There are many things that raise my eyebrows as an adult with regard to bullying, but I will focus on just a couple here and you're free to hear my other concerns during my self-esteem and personal growth speaking engagements.

I believe that I took the stance of becoming a bully rather than being bullied because I come from a family where we spoke up for ourselves, we "ranked" on each other on a regular basis and if you could not spontaneously "rank" on someone, that in and of itself was a rank. We said whatever we thought without wondering about consequences and for those who were sensitive, they were deemed to be "punks" and that was an unacceptable position to hold in my family. This was not just my immediate family, but my extended family as well. So, having pity on myself when someone said something unfavorable was not an option. Getting beat up was also not an option because you could not come home and tell anyone, parents included, that someone hit you and you did nothing about it. If you won the fight, cool, but if you did not, that meant you had to go back and this time with cousins, they'd let you fight "fair" but if someone else jumped in that was it.

I try to find the positive from all actions. While some can relate to what I've described, there will be some who cannot. I can say that I have learned to channel the bullying attitude into working hard, going after what I want, standing up for what I believe in, and believe it or not, sitting in the front of the class is something I do now wherever I am because that has taught me that you receive the best energy from the front, you're almost certain to receive the handouts before they run out, the first to receive, have a better

6

chance of getting your questions answered and so much more. I know that God gives us all a disposition, but it is our obligation to righteously refine it. Therefore, we should by no means pursue the replication of others. By seeking to do so means (1) that God made a mistake in choosing to uniquely create you and you're stating you could have created a better specimen and (2) if you were successful in becoming the other person that you seek to emulate, what happens when they seek to emulate someone else, does that mean, yet, another chase for you and (3) If you were successful at transitioning into that person, then there is only need for one of you. We all like designer clothing, jewelry, cars, etc. Well, I am a designer original, made by the ultimate designer, God! The difference with my designer is He never duplicates a design, so you can only find me, when you interact with ME! The same holds true for you!

It also occurred to me, much later, in life, that it is imperative that we monitor, closely who and what we choose to surround ourselves. This is not only from a face-to-face standpoint, but also from the television, music, reading material, and so on. I believe that the three people that you hang out with, influence your thinking. I used to always tell my son, show me your friends and I will tell you who you are.

With regard to my bout with low self-esteem, I cannot help but think that if I suffered from the possession of a low self-esteem and I have two loving, not perfect, but loving parents, it is magnified by 20 for those who do not have engaged parents. I choose the term "engaged" because I am of the mindset that all parents love their children, but not all parents know how to parent, nor express love. This book is for all girls because all people suffer from a low self-esteem at some point. However girls have different manners in which we suffer from low self-esteem. The preeminent difference is that girls grow to become women and women become mothers and mothers are the birthing canal from which all life form flows, which means we are the first teachers of everyone. Change a girl, change a world.

So, I've said all of that to say, I can only attempt to imagine what girls who do not have both parents, in today's society, are facing. Additionally, not only do some not have parents, but we live in a society where adults have been scared of our youth and will refuse to correct ill behavior, may be in a position where they are battling an addiction, or some other major areas of concern – double whammy!

This book serves three purposes: (1) to **teach** girls, tweens, teens, young ladies, young adults, and parents how to define what self-esteem looks like. As an educator, it is incumbent upon me to decode ambiguity, whenever possible, especially to those who are engaging for the first time. For example, if I tell you to clean your room, in my mind that looks one way, in the mind of a three year old, a clean room looks like something else. This will cause frustration for both people. However, if I say to the three year old, or the person who is now being charged with the task of cleaning her room for the first time, to make her bed and show her how to execute accomplishing the making of a bed, complete with hospital corners, properly hanging up clothes, dusting furniture, placing shoes in boxes, etc. then the person being told what to do will know that her just throwing the covers over the bed will not suffice. Same premise applies to self-esteem. Girls need to know what it looks like before they can execute it. **The second purpose: (2)** how to **execute** their newly acquired or enhanced positive self-esteem. Once girls, tweens, teens, young ladies, young adults, and parents are able to assuredly define self-esteem is when one is also able to implement it. One can only apply what she has truly learned. And **the final, purpose: (3)** how to **maintain** self-esteem. Procurement is easier than maintenance. It is easy to make a friend, but maintaining the friendship, especially when other variables, such as other friends, boyfriends, cousins, after school activities, etc. come into play can strain friendships and relationships. However, when you are secure in who you are regardless of external forces is when you are a better friend, daughter, sister, student, and overall person. Guess what? Looks play less of a role than we are made to believe. Please do not confuse having a positive and healthy self-esteem with being conceited – they are NOT related whatsoever.

You will learn how to detect qualities of a healthy self-esteem in yourself and others. You will also realize that we all have "not so good" days. While there is no pinnacle as we, as humans, can always improve, when you begin to more frequently experience a place where you are comfortable with exuding self-confidence free of arrogance without having to be critical of others, you know you are on the right path. The life of a person with high self-esteem is really a different life...it is what I refer to as "The Good Life!" You will accept yourself as you are (the things you cannot change) and you accept others as they are, which means that people feel good being and wanting to be around you.

Do you sincerely want to feel better about yourself? Do you want cultivate healthy relationships? Do you want to know how to become a good friend? Do you want to reap all the benefits that having a healthy self-esteem provides? Do you want to build a healthy relationship with your daughter/granddaughter/niece? If you answered, "yes" to one or all of the above questions, this is the book for you! This book will transform your life for the rest of your life. How do I know? I know because I was where you are, suffering from a low self-esteem, however, with work, I have transformed my life. While we all have days where we are not feeling the most confident, beautiful, smart, etc., but when a day turns into a month, a year or two, therein lies a major concern. This book, if followed will assist you in your transformation. Studies show that it takes at least 66 consecutive days before something becomes a habit. You will be able to reach the 90% mark as you utilize this book more and more in the intended manner. As a result you will teach others, just by being good to yourself, first. Remember, you teach others how to interact with you, by virtue of how you first treat yourself. Go forth and become the spectacular person you were created to be.

Certified by New York State Office of Children & Family Services Bridges to Health (B2H) Home & Community Board Services Medicaid Waiver Program in Crisis Services, Safety, Essential Elements for Service Provision, Building Resilience, Planned & Crisis, CPR, First Aid, Respite, Skill Building, Family Care Giver Support Services (Parenting Skills), & Documentation. I am providing some of the information that we use within our Child Development Guide (NYSOCFS Bureau of Training Division of Development & Prevention Services through the center for Development of Human Services Research of SUNY Buffalo State College). In Appendix I – (great resource for parents – see the developmental guide from ages eight to 19).

How to be a Young Lady
Your Total Guide for Being the Best Possible You!

Chapter One

Affirmations

"And whatsoever we ask, we receive of Him, because we keep His commandments, and do those things that are pleasing in His sight."
~1 John 3:22

Affirmations

Affirmations are a group of words that we say to ourselves that are positive. Along with saying these words, we must believe them. It is okay if this exercise is new for you and you do not believe the words yet. This is referred to as cognitive dissonance (the state of having inconsistent thoughts, beliefs, or attitudes as relating to behavioral decisions and attitude change), however, for the purposes of this book, in effort of getting you to the next level, we'll refer to it as the "fake it until you make it" concept. Whichever term you choose, I'm more concerned that you apply it.

You can say these words with positive music and or positive pictures, while looking into the mirror or walking down the street. Think of affirmations as a form of self-talk. Self-talk is what we say to and about ourselves coupled with what we think about ourselves. For example, if someone says that you are pretty and you do not think you are pretty – what stands out more? Yes, what you believe is what stands out most. If you do not think you are pretty, what others say seem like a contradiction to what you already believe, thus their words do not matter. To make certain that they know how you feel, you will probably respond with a negative comment rather than simply saying, thank you.

Below are a few affirmations to get you started and then you will think of some affirmations about yourself that you like:

I am beautiful on the inside
I am beautiful on the outside
I will be in touch with my feelings about me
I am important
I am special
I will strive to be better, today
I am getting better every single moment
I feel better, so life is better
I am someone that no one else can be
I love me
I am beautiful because I exist
I am a designer original, no one is like me
There is no one like me
I am a unique and beautiful creation
My thoughts are a reflection of how I see others and the world
I will forgive me
I will forgive others
I love and approve of myself
All that I need is waiting for me
I cannot change yesterday, so I embrace today
I make the choice to love me
Happiness is learning something new
Happiness is being teachable
I am better today than yesterday
I am smarter today than yesterday
Happiness is being able to learn new things
Happiness is being humble
Happiness is knowing right from wrong and choosing to do what is right

2

Happiness is loving who I am
Happiness is knowing that there is no one exactly like me, I am unique
Happiness is associating with positive peers
Happiness is choosing to obey my parents
Happiness is finding wisdom and gaining understanding
Happiness is recognizing peace
Happiness is organizing my path
Happiness is choosing to build a healthy lifestyle
Happiness is knowing that happiness is a choice that I have chosen

Your turn. Write some affirmations that you have come up with:

1)

2)

3)

4)

5)

6)

7)

8)

9)

10)

11)

12)

13)

14)

15)

16)

17)

18)

19)

20)

Chapter Two

Mirror Mirror on the Wall

"My child, listen closely to My teachings and learn common sense."
~Proverbs 4:1

Mirror Mirror on the Wall Cards

Below is a one month supply of affirmations to place on index cards. Place the index card on your mirror to recite each day. Remember, our self-talk is very important. Place a card on your mirror the night before and in the morning, the first person that you see is a positive person. YOU! Guess what?! These work great on days that you get up on the "wrong side of the bed". Use the card that most reflects how you are feeling. You may find that one particular card is up more than another. Try it for yourself and see.

Day 1: Do not worry about anything, instead, pray about everything. Tell God what I need, and thank Him for all He has done. ~Philippians 4:6

Day 2: Then, because I belong to Christ Jesus, God will bless me with peace that no one can completely understand. And this peace will control the way I think and feel. ~Philippians 4:7

Day 3: I can do ALL things through Christ who strengthens me. ~Philippians 4:13

Day 4: The Sovereign Lord is my strength; He makes my feet like the feet of a deer, He enables me to go on the heights. ~Habakkuk **3:19**

Day 5: the Lord is my light and my salvation; whom shall I fear? The Lord is the strength of my life; of whom shall I be afraid? Wait on the Lord: be of good courage, and He shall strengthen my heart: wait, I say, on the Lord. ~Psalm 27: 1-14

Day 6: The Lord is my Rock, and my Fortress, and my Deliverer; my God, my strength, in who I will trust: He is my shield, the strength of my salvation, and my high tower. ~Psalm 18:2

Day 7: Be of good courage, and He shall strengthen my heart, all of us that hope in the Lord. ~Psalm 31:24

Day 8: The Lord protects the upright but destroys the wicked. ~Proverbs 10:29

Day 9: Counsel is mine, and sound wisdom I Am understanding; I have strength. ~Proverbs 8:14

Day 10: See, God has come to save me. I will trust in Him and not be afraid. The Lord God is my strength and my song; He has become my salvation. ~Isaiah 12:2

Day 11: A wise girl is mightier than a strong girl, and a girl of knowledge is more powerful than a strong girl.

Day 12: I will lie down in peace and sleep for you alone, O Lord, will keep me safe. ~Psalm 4:8

Day 13: Those that are gentle and lowly will possess the land: they will live in prosperous security.

Day 14: Be still in the presence of the Lord, and wait patiently for Him to act. Don't worry about evil people who prosper or worry about their wicked schemes. ~Psalm 37:7

Day 15: Stop my anger! Turn from my rage! Do not envy others – it only leads to harm.

Day 16: It is better to be Godly and have little than to be evil and possess much. ~Psalm 37:16

Day 17: Take delight in the Lord, and He will give me my heart's desires. ~Psalm 37:4

Day 18: Blessed are the merciful; for they shall obtain mercy. ~Matthew 5:7

Day 19: Love my enemies, bless them that curse me, do good to them that hate me, and pray for them which despitefully use me, and persecute me. ~Matthew 5:44

Day 20: The Lord is my shepherd; I shall not want. ~Psalm 23:1

Day 21: For God hath not given me a spirit of fear; but of power, and of love, and of a sound mind. ~II Timothy 1:67

Day 22: If I love sleep, I will end up in poverty. Keep my eyes open and there will be plenty to eat!

Day 23: Finishing is better than starting, patience is better than pride.

Day 24: Don't be quick tempered, for anger is the friend of fools.

Day 25: Wisdom or money can get me almost anything, but it's important to know that only wisdom can save my life.

Day 26: If I wait for perfect conditions, I will never get anything done.

Day 27: Obey the teachings of my parents, and wear their teachings as I would a lovely hat or a pretty necklace. Don't be tempted by sinners... ~Proverbs 1:8-10

Day 28: Let love and loyalty always show like a necklace, and write them in my mind.

Day 29: God blesses everyone who has wisdom and common sense. Wisdom is worth more than silver; it makes me much richer than gold. Wisdom is worth more than silver; it makes me much richer than gold. Wisdom is more valuable than precious jewels; nothing I want compares with her. Wisdom makes life pleasant and leads me safely along. Wisdom is a life-giving tree, the source of happiness for all who hold on to her. ~Proverbs 3:13-15; 17-18

Day 30: My road won't be blocked, and I won't stumble when I run. Hold firmly to God's teaching and never let go, it will mean life for me. Don't follow the bad example of cruel and evil people. ~Proverbs 4:12-14

Day 31: What if I could speak all languages of humans and of angels? If I did not love others I would be nothing more than a noisy gong or a clanging cymbal. What if I could prophesy and understand all secrets and all knowledge? And what if I had faith and moved mountains? I would be nothing, unless I loved others. What if I gave away all that I owned and let myself be burned alive? I would gain nothing unless I loved others. Love is kind and patient, never jealous, boastful, proud or rude. Love isn't selfish or quick tempered. It doesn't keep a record of wrongs that others do. Love rejoices in the truth, but not in evil. Love is always supportive, loyal, hopeful, and trusting. Love never fails! Everyone who prophecies will stop and unknown languages will no longer be spoken. All that we know will be forgotten. We don't know everything and our prophecies are not complete. But what is perfect will someday appear, and what isn't perfect will then disappear. When we were children, we thought and reasoned as children do. But when we grew up we quit our childish ways. Now all we can see of God is like a cloudy picture in a mirror. Later we will see Him face-to-face. We don't know everything, but then we will, just as God completely understands us. For now there are faith, hope, and love. But of these three, the greatest is LOVE.

~I Corinthians 13

Chapter Three

The Ultimate Love Story

"Be wise and learn good sense, remember My teachings and do what I say."
Proverbs 4:5

The Ultimate Love Story

As Jacob continued on his way to the east, he looked out in a field and saw a well where shepherds took their sheep for water. Three flocks of sheep were lying around the well, which was covered with a large rock. Shepherds would roll the rock away when all their sheep had gathered there. Then after the sheep had been watered the shepherds would roll the rock back over the mouth of the well.

Jacob asked the shepherds, "Where are you from?" We're from Haran, "they answered. Then he asked, "Do you know Nahor's grandson, Laban?" "Yes, we do," they replied. "How is he?' Jacob asked. "He is fine," they answered. "And here comes his daughter, Rachel, with the sheep."

Jacob told them, "Look, the sun is still high up in the sky, and it's too early to bring in the rest of the flocks. Water your sheep and take them back to the pasture."

But they replied, "We can't do that until they all get here, and the rock has been rolled away from the well." While Jacob was still talking with the men, his cousin Rachel came up with her father's sheep. When Jacob saw her and his uncle's sheep, he rolled the rock away and watered the sheep.

He then kissed Rachel and started crying because he was so happy. He told her that he was the son of her aunt Rebekah, and she ran and told her father about him. As soon as Laban heard the news, he ran out to meet Jacob. He hugged and kissed him and brought him to his home, where Jacob told him everything that had happened. Laban said, "You are my nephew and you are like one of my own family."

11

After Jacob had been there for a month, Laban said to him, "You shouldn't have to work without pay just because you are a relative of mine. What do you want me to give you?" Laban had two daughters. Leah was older than Rachel, but her eyes didn't sparkle, while Rachel was beautiful and had a good figure. Since Jacob was in love with Rachel, he answered, "If you will let me marry Rachel, I'll work seven years for you." Laban replied, "It's better for me to let you marry Rachel than for someone else to have her. So stay and work for me. "Jacob worked seven years for Laban, but the time seemed like only a few days, because he loved Rachel so much. Jacob said to Laban, "The time is up, and I want to marry Rachel now!"

So Laban gave a big feast and invited all their neighbors. But that event he brought Leah to Jacob, who married her and spent the night with her. Laban also gave Zilpha to Leah as her servant woman.

The next morning Jacob found out that he had married Leah, and he asked Laban, "Why did you do this to me? Didn't I work to get Rachel? Why did you trick me?"

Laban replied, in our country the older daughter must get married first. After you spend this week with Leah, you may also marry Rachel. But you will have to work for me another seven years.

At the end of the week of celebration, Laban let Jacob marry Rachel, and he gave her his servant woman Bilhah Jacob loved Rachel more than he did Leah, but he had to work another seven years for Laban.

12

The Lord knew that Jacob loved Rachel more than he did Leah, and so he gave children to Leah, but not to Rachel. Leah gave birth to a son and named him Reuben, because she said, "The Lord has taken away my sorrow. Now my husband will love me more than he does Rachel." She had a second son and named him Simeon, because she said, "The Lord has heard that my husband doesn't love me." When Leah's third son was born, she said," now my husband will hold me close." So this son was named Levi. She had one more son and named him Judah, because she said, "I'll praise the Lord!"

Rachel eventually was blessed with children.

There are several things that I hope you have learned from this excerpt, however, list what you have learned and then match them with my answers below.

I have learned (feel free to add more, if you like):

1)
2)
3)
4)
5)
6)
7)
8)
9)
10)

_____

_____

_____

_____

Answers:

1. Know the rules to the game before you agree to play

2. Get it in writing, i.e., marriage certificate

3. Laban loved Rachel so much that he was willing to wait for her in every manner, including sexually.

4. Refrain from becoming intoxicated with alcohol or drugs, as it will cloud your ability to think appropriately

5. Do not ever believe that having a baby, or two, or three, etc. will hold a boy/man, it did not work in ancient Biblical days and will not work in modern day society

6. When a man loves a woman, he is not willing to force her to do anything immoral

7. A man that loves a woman is willing to bend over backward to assist with her happiness

8. A boy man will still have sex with you even though he does not love you – don't equate sex with love.

Here are some questions for those of you who think you're in love:

1. Are you mentally prepared to deal with what sex presents? Do you even know what it represents and presents? If you're confused about this question, your answer is, "NO!"

2. Should a child be conceived, are you ready mentally, psychologically, and financially? I do mean independent of your parents.

3. Are you prepared to sacrifice friends, after school sports, and other fun things to take care of a baby?

4. Are you ready to deal with the consequences of contracting a fatal or any kind of sexually transmitted disease?

5. What will happen to your child in the event you contract a deadly sexually transmitted disease or other illness that leads to your death?

6. Are you prepared to confront issues that come with caring for a child? How about a child with a disability? How about when the child gets older and his/her peers tease him/her about his/her disability?

7. Are you prepared to become a single parent?

Please be honest with your answers and give them some "REAL" thought. I trust you will believe that parenting is for mature adults who have made a conscious decision to bring a life into this world. Even in that case, parenting can be difficult, at best.

Children are born with "clean slates"; think about what you will be able to engrave onto a child's slate, right now, that would give them a positive start at this thing called life.

Chapter Four

The Basics

"…Good sense is more important than anything else. If I value Wisdom and hold tightly to her, great honors will be mine. It will be like wearing a glorious crown of beautiful flowers."
~Proverbs 4:7-9

The Basics

Etiquette is what everyone needs for different occasions. For instance, your etiquette at the dinner table will be different than the etiquette that is needed for an outing at the park, while sitting on a blanket with food in a basket.

There is a time when primary etiquette is needed in all arenas. An example of primary etiquette would be the manner in which a lady carries herself. A lady is a lady in all arenas. A lady should always behave in a manner that commands unspoken respect. Let us think about this for a moment – the manner in which you carry (behave) yourself is a weeding out process. If your thoughts, words, and actions are those of respect, people that are not interested in respect will usually not befriend you. That is a good thing! Now you do not need to waste your precious time figuring them out. You may now utilize your time in a more productive manner.

A YOUNG LADY & HER FRIENDS
A Young Lady Should:

use her manners every day, even with people that she does not fancy.

never talk about one friend to another.

be supportive of her friend's accomplishments and not envy them.

remember to be in control of her thoughts and words so that she will not be offensive to her friends.

know that real friends want what is good for her.

remember that a lady that exudes inner beauty will not miss an opportunity to genuinely show kindness to her family and friends.

remember that saying the right thing at the right time is one of the greatest things a lady can do for herself and others.
know that appropriately timed silence can be a great asset.

remember that God gave her two ears and one mouth, so that she can do more listening than talking.
know that friends with good parents have rules, also.

A YOUNG LADY & COURTING
A Young Lady Should:

be of proper age before courting. Recommendation: age 17
have her family's permission to court.

know his family. You should not be a secret. If he's hiding you, he's ashamed of you.

have introduced him to her family. Same rule above, applies.

have introduced her family to his family.

should have a chaperone or go out in groups that stay together for the entire date.

know that courting for any length of time does not entitle her to engage in any sexual activity, whatsoever.

consult her parents about intimacy.

alert her parents or a trusted adult if she is being mistreated in any manner.

recognize that males are different from females. This does not make her or him better, it just makes each different.

know that she must be comfortable with herself first. never expect him to be her "end all, be all".

still have positive relationships with her female friends.

know that when they are walking down the street, he should be on the side closest to the sidewalk.

not entertain the company of a young man who indulges in drugs and/or alcohol.

not entertain the company of a young man who lacks manners.

not entertain the company of a young man who does not know when to dress appropriately for the occasion.

not entertain the company of a young man who does not respect his parents.

not entertain the company of a young man who brags about fighting.

be observant of his friend's behavior, attitude, manners, and treatment of young ladies.

Darlene Aiken

A YOUNG LADY AS A HOUSEGUEST
A Young Lady Should:

remove her shoes upon arrival if it is raining, snowing, or inclement weather.

appropriately hang up her coat in the closet if the hostess has not, never throw it on the floor or drape it over the sofa.

always greet others that are in the home already.

follow the agenda of the hostess.

never wander apart from other guests.

refrain from going into the refrigerator and cupboards without permission.

wait for the hostess to announce when the meal will be served.

wait until she is asked if she is hungry.

ask before using the telephone and never make long distance calls.

excuse herself if she need to use her cell phone to make an important call, unrelated to being there.

always wear a bathrobe to and from the bathroom, if she's spent the night.

make her bed immediately upon rising.

get dressed as soon as possible, especially if there is only one bathroom.

keep her designated area neat and tidy when visiting.

not stay up too late, when the hostess has to rise early.

not sleep too late.

assist with the dishes and light chores without being asked.

A YOUNG LADY & HYGIENE
A Young Lady Should:

always bathe before leaving the house.

always bathe upon rising, even if she does not plan to leave the house.

take more baths than showers as her vaginal area needs to soak.

always wear clean and appropriately fitting undergarments without the

aid of safety pins of any sort.

know that she should never neglect to thoroughly wash behind her ears and carefully clean her navel, to avoid hidden odors.

drink plenty of filtered water.

make regular gynecology appointments, when it becomes age appropriate.

implement exercise into her weekly routine.

develop healthy eating habits.

refrain from wearing underpants that do not have a cotton crotch.

carry tiny breath mints at all times, never chew gum in public.

always have tissues in her purse.

carry hand sanitizer in her purse.

dispose of sanitary napkins and tampons discreetly.

thoroughly wash hands with soap often.

know that hand sanitizer does not take the place of hand washing.

never sit on public toilets. If she must, then line them with paper towels first, but never flush the paper towels.

wash hands before and after using the toilet.

never wear pajamas in public, it gives the appearance that you did not wash.

always wipe from the front to the back and not the reverse, to avoid the transferring of bacteria.

should refrain from using colored toilet tissue, whenever, possible. The tissue in your purse will come in handy when in this situation.

brush and floss her teeth after every meal, whenever possible.

whenever possible, refrain from flushing the toilet while still sitting as bacteria floats upward into the vagina.
always carry a purse sized bottle of perfume and spray before leaving the public bathroom stall.

A YOUNG LADY'S PUBLIC IMAGE
A Young Lady Should:

dress appropriately for the occasion.

know that wearing undergarments only in public is inappropriate and unladylike.

know that wearing pajamas, slippers, hair curlers, & soiled scarves in public, gives the impression that she has extremely poor hygiene.

know that wearing rags on her head to cover up a bad hair day is inappropriate.

take time to style her hair.

know that when her backside is sticking out of her shorts or

skirt that she is not behaving as a lady.

know that, in general, ladies are seen and not heard. Loud women in public are disgraceful.

24

smile often.

refrain from walking the street at night, whenever possible.

refrain from getting into a street argument and/or fight.

know that when she crosses the street she should lift the leg furthest from the sidewalk first, elevate herself to lift the next leg and come up to the sidewalk because a lady always keeps her legs crossed.

know when getting into a car or Sports Utility Vehicle (SUV), she should put her legs together, sit, and then bring legs around into the vehicle all at once.

keep her legs together or crossed when she is sitting down, even if she has on pants.

learn how to be social in any setting.
not drink alcohol.

never leave her beverage unattended under any circumstances.

refrain from making an appearance as or with an uninvited guest.

compliment another young lady who has an identical or similar outfit.

not wear too much perfume. *Hint*: if you still smell it long after you have left the house, you have on too much and it stinks to others.

never wear old perfume or make-up. *Hint*: if you've had it over two years, discard, immediately.

not bring gifts that have been used to someone else. remove the price tags before wrapping.

not buy inexpensive gifts from inexpensive stores and wrap gifts in wrapping paper & boxes from expensive stores.

not purchase unattractive or gifts that she would not buy for herself to give to others.

never smoke anything! Nuff said!

refrain from using fowl language.

not eat ice cream cones in public. Use a spoon.

never permit anyone to disrespect her.

A YOUNG LADY & SELF-ESTEEM
A Young Lady Should:

first define herself, therefore, she does not fall prey to the erroneous definitions that others may apply. One of the germane reasons for having a healthy self-esteem.

always seek to establish exceptional etiquette skills, forever.

remember to include positive affirmations in her daily

regimen.

set positive short and long-term goals.

constructively criticize herself, this is the building process.

refrain from negative self-talk. This is different from constructive criticism. For example, negative talk solely focuses on her downfall without presenting positive solutions.
work toward eliminating negative people from her inner circle.

know that when she operates in a manner that builds her self-esteem, she allows her blessings to flow.

remember that her life is a reflection of her choices.

remember to be selective of who she refers to as "friends".

remember that when people are jealous of her, it's simply, confused admiration.

remember that she can learn from her enemies. This includes how "not" to treat others and what not to do.

be in control of her thoughts, at all times.

remember that control is either internal or external – either she will control herself, or others will be forced to do so from their standpoint.

feed herself with as much positive information as possible.

seek to turn a negative into a positive.

think before acting, as some actions are irreversible and the same is true for some of the consequences as a result of her actions.

remember that it is her responsibility to define and seek happiness.

relieve herself of stress by exercising, organizing, and prioritizing what is important to her.

learn how and when to say, "no" & understand that it's important to exercise this right when appropriate.

assess and continually reassess her needs and change old ways of responding.

reject things and/or people who no longer appropriately serve her needs in helping procure and/or maintain her positive self-esteem.

depend on herself to motivate and empower herself.

seek quality first, in all that she engages in and trust that quantity will come.

remember that she is a unique gift to the world with unique talents and gifts.

remember that her talents and gifts are not for her, but for others, so to not use, improve upon, nor sharing them, cuts the world off from what she brings.

know that it's not necessarily good just because "everyone is doing it!"

knows that it's okay to be alone and not feel lonely.

know that it's necessary to get to know herself.

A LADY & COMMUNICATION
A Young Lady Should:

try to avoid becoming involved in loud arguments.

listen for an opportunity to agree to compromise.

try to develop fair solutions to situations so that she and the other person may both end up in a winning situation.
think before she speaks.

focus more on having compassion for others than seeking compassion for one's self.

always remember to be polite when speaking and/or interacting with others.

know that speaking ill of someone does not divulge their negativity, but divulges her negative image.

ask for clarity when she does not understand something and not fear being "dumb".

not interrupt when someone else is speaking.

refrain from saying, "I know" while someone is speaking.

use eye contact and other appropriate forms of body language to show that she is focused and listening.

give a firm, not a "wet noodle" or tightly squeezed handshake.

CLEANLINESS IS NEXT TO GODLINESS
A Young Lady Should:

make up her bed every morning.

never sit on or sleep in her bed with clothes that she wore in the street.

dust and vacuum at least once per week, most of the dust is caused by dead skin from your body and this may cause allergies and asthma.

wash her bed pillow at least twice per month. If the pillow is non-washable, disinfect it by spraying it with a disinfectant and sitting it in the sun for an hour rotating 30 minutes on each side (change at least every two years).

know that her pillow accumulates a percentage of old dead skin which promotes an environment for dust mites and their excrement along with mold. Couple that with saliva, hair, hair oils (natural and added), facial creams, lotions, perfume, etc. sounds disgusting? It is! This may also contribute to illness, acne, as well as an uncontrollable odor in her room.

vacuum her mattress at least once per month as it, also, accumulates dead skin from the body and could cause allergies and other reactions.

wash her hands thoroughly – always using warm soapy water, wash hands, wrists, palms, in between fingers, backs of hands and do not forget to get under her rings and fingernails. Do this until she finishes reciting the alphabet. Dry hands with disposable paper towels – *note*: always roll the paper towel down before washing her hands, pat your hands thoroughly, **keep** some lotion nearby, and, oh! Use liquid soap whenever possible.

keep her closet neat, all blouses together, pants, skirts, etc. all hangers should hang in the same direction as should clothes-for example, the front of two shirts should not be facing one another.

keep her shoes stored properly, keep them in their original box (if possible) or buy shoe boxes.

PREPARATIONS BEFORE COOKING.
A Young Lady Should:

always get permission from her parents, if she is too young, to operate the stove.

wash hands thoroughly (see above) this is to ensure that you do not contaminate food and partakers of the food.

prepare fresh dishwater so that you can clean as you go. This makes the clean up easier.

clean her work area so that unnecessary clutter may be avoided. As she finishes with a particular item, put it away.

read the recipe before cooking. This will allow her to know which ingredients she needs before beginning to cook.

put on an apron to prevent clothes from becoming soiled.

TABLE MANNERS
A Young Lady Should:

always be on time for dinner.

pull her chair closer to the table and sit up straight.

place her napkin on her lap.

not begin to eat until everyone has been served, especially the host

talk freely at the table, but never with her mouth full of food.

not watch television or listen to the radio during mealtime.

use mealtime as an opportunity to talk to her family.

know the difference between an informal table setting and a formal table setting.

never lean on her elbows at the table.

know that at a formal table setting, the food is not served all at one time, but is brought out and taken away to make room for the next course selection.

know that at the restaurant the following occurs:
appetizers are first.
salad is the second course.
the third course is the entrée (pronounced on-tray) and this is usually served with vegetables, rice or

potatoes.
dessert, tea, and coffee are served last.

know that it is appropriate to use her fingers with finger foods only.

know that it is inappropriate to use utensils for most finger foods.

know that some finger foods include:
tacos, fried chicken, fried fish, watermelon, and other hand held fruits, such as grapes, pizza, frankfurters, pickles, and asparagus.

know that there are some difficult to handle foods, such as lobster, shish kebabs, spaghetti, cherry tomatoes, peas, soups, and salads.

know that she should use her nutcracker to open the lobster shell and pick the lobster out with the lobster fork.

use her knife to assist the peas onto her fork.

cut her salad into pieces, as she goes, rather than forcing large leaves into her mouth.

not stab, but pierce the cherry tomato, cut it and then eat it.

place the tip of the skewer on to her plate, hold the top end

with her hand and then take her fork and slide her meat, veggies, etc. off into her plate. Once on the plate, cut the large pieces and eat.

use a spaghetti spoon while winding her spaghetti with her fork.

not slurp her soup or blow it when it is hot, rather, let it cool before eating.

never lick her fingers!

never blow her nose at the dinner table. However, if her nose is running,

dab with a tissue from her purse and excuse herself and go to the restroom.

never use the napkin at the table, especially the cloth napkin.

HELPFUL TIDBITS FOR A YOUNG LADY
A Young Lady Should:

always send a neatly handwritten thank you note after someone or several have shown an act of kindness.

never tell someone something that is embarrassing when they are incapable of changing the embarrassment, immediately.

be honest when a friend asks about her hair or attire before they're going out.

know that it is inappropriate for an older man to make advances at her. Therefore, it's not a compliment.

know that it is NEVER wrong for her to tell, if ANY male touches her in an inappropriate manner. She should never believe that it is her fault. Always tell a trusting adult.

Darlene Aiken

never cry rape if she was not!

never lie about her age.

never sit on a man's lap.

never wear a shirt with words written across her chest and buttocks.

never invite two or more boys/young men, at the same time, to meet her at her house to go out.

know that extremely long fingernails are a sign of an unkempt young lady, as she's unable to wash the "hot spots" appropriately.

know that if she chooses to wear a wig or weave in public, she should comb it and put it on straight and keep it neat.

know that if she is of age to wear makeup, that she should not recreate only enhance herself.

only wear makeup when it is age appropriate.

be wise enough to not let anyone who has been drinking and/or drugging drive her anyplace.

be wise enough to know that she should NEVER indulge in TWD – Texting While Driving.

consider volunteering her time with a reputable community or faith-based organization, especially when she is feeling down.

EMPLOYMENT
A Young Lady Should:

become knowledgeable about the company that she is seeking employment.

have an idea about the questions that she would like to ask, based on her research.

always give a firm handshake, this shows interest.

answer questions in a truthful manner and to the point. have good hygiene and appearance.

only wear clear fingernail polish, as colors tend to mark documents.

not wear loud perfume, lotions and/or grooming oils.

make sure her lip gloss is not extremely shiny.

wear her hair in a professional bun or bob.
keep jewelry simple, no medallions, name earrings, nose rings, flashy and/or multiple rings, tongue rings, lip rings, eyebrow rings, etc.

not wear loud chemically colored hair i.e., electric blue with pink streaks, etc.

leave video type clothes, hairdo's and accessories at home, better yet, leave them in the store, remember you are a lady at all times.

possess the ability to express herself clearly – strong voice, diction, and grammar.

possess confidence (this comes with preparation and healthy self-esteem).

possess poise.

not be ill-mannered.

not chew gum even if the interviewer is chewing gum.

not smoke even if the interviewer is smoking or offers you a cigarette.

look the interviewer in the eyes.

not turn in a sloppy application.

read the application first, then neatly complete the appropriate areas.

not arrive late to the interview – however, sometimes circumstances do arise, so she should have the telephone number and name of the contact person in her purse/phone to call as soon as she recognizes that a concern is ensuing.

always give a time that will allow her to be on time, as to call a second time to say that she is *still* going to be late, is unacceptable and raises eyebrows with regard to her seriousness for the position.

attempt to obtain the name of the person(s) that will interview her.

never use her cell phone while waiting to be interviewed, this includes texting.

bring an intellectual book to read to pass the time.

place her phone on "quiet" mode or turn off completely.

have on hand the following: her social security card, birth certificate, passport, names, addresses, and telephone numbers of at least five updated references. Updated means that you've asked their permission to use them as references.

greet the receptionist with a smile and a firm handshake. upon leaving, thank the receptionist for her assistance and show kindness by saying, "have a nice day."

know that business attire should be black, navy blue, dark brown, or business gray.

know that business attire is professional regardless of the nature of the position.
not bring friends, relatives, boyfriends, etc. to the interview.

have the person that is driving her to the interview stay in the car and wait until she comes out.

not use slang on her application nor in the body of the interview.

acknowledge those that she knows who may be applying for the job, but do not sit next to them and hold a conversation.

not speak in a negative manner about former employers or co-workers to the interviewer.

know how to creatively, without lying, speak about her reason(s) for leaving a prior job, especially if the separation was unfavorable.

not assume that she can dress down for the interview just because everyone who works there is not dressed up.

not say that she has skills, education, or something that she does not have.

not eat a breakfast that includes garlic, onions, or anything that will make her breath unfavorable.

Checklist to use before she goes on an interview:

_____Did I research the company and the job responsibilities?

_____Did I go over some of the questions that may be asked?

_____Did I go over some of the questions that I may ask?

_____How will I get to the interview?

_____How will I get home from the interview?

_____What time must I leave in order to arrive on time?

_____How is my attitude?

_____Do I have five updated references?

_____Is my resume updated?

_____Do I have the appropriate clothes for the interview?

Darlene Aiken

Making the Best Impression on an Interview

Fashion Tips from Celebrity Fashion Stylist and Image Consultant, Carlton Spence

Ladies, being prepared for an interview is very important. However, your presentation, how you look, and what you wear are equally important. Here are some helpful fashion tips that will ensure that you look your very best. When you feel and look good, you will exude confidence. After all, you have one opportunity to make a first impression.

Hair – Whether your hair is natural or permed, short or long, choose a hairstyle that is not trendy, but classic and sophisticated. Avoid too much hairspray and chemically colored hair. Also, do not wear any hair ornaments or accessories, such as rhinestone hair pins.

Makeup – Apply your makeup to achieve a flawless and natural look with a dewy lip. Wear lipstick or lip gloss that is closest to your natural lip color. Avoid wearing red lipstick. Save that for a special occasion, if you are old enough for lipstick – recommendation – 17 and up (fix your face; you have all your life to be an adult, preserve your youthfulness as long as possible).

Nails – If your budget allows, treat yourself to a professional manicure. Nail polish should be neutral or clear in color. Do not wear bright colored nail polish and avoid French tips. Nails should be clean and cut short, as in business length.

Perfume – Wear your signature fragrance that is not over-powering. Gingerly spray perfume on your pulse points and never spray perfume directly on your clothing. Also, make certain your perfume is not old.

Shape wear – Finding the perfect fitting bra can be an arduous task. Visit your local department store and inquire about a complimentary bra fitting at the lingerie department. Determining the right bra for your body type and size will make you look and feel your best.

If your shape is curvy or full figured, wear Spanx (shaper or tights) to enhance your shape and ensure a smooth fit.

Jewelry – Opt to wear minimal and classic jewelry. Examples of this are: small posts or small hoop earrings. Avoid wearing necklaces with bold, large pendants. Wedding and/or engagement rings are appropriate. Do not wear multiple rings or stacked rings. Gold or silver, sleek and modern watch is appropriate. Avoid wearing stacked bracelets or bangles, as they make noise and are distracting during an interview.

BASIC SURVIVAL WARDROBE
Do's and Don'ts By Celebrity Fashion Stylist & Image Consultant, Carlton Spence
A Young Lady Should:

Consider the list below as her first pieces of business attire:

Blazer/Jacket – (see business colors above). Your blazer/jacket should be solid, no stripes, checks, or any other pattern. While you do not have to spend tons of money on it, the quality should be good. This will give you many years of use, which ultimately saves money in the long run. Refrain from latest trends, as they go out of style. Always choose conservative, as this transcends time. Wool or wool blends for the colder months and linen, cotton or silk blends for spring and summer. Also, many of us have favorite designers, however, please tear the designer label off your blazer/jacket before wearing, it is not fashionable. Always wear appropriate underwear, it makes a difference.

Sweaters – are versatile because they supplement the wardrobe for suits, skirts, business slacks, etc. Sweaters may be thick in texture or light, depending the season you are wearing them. They should not be tight and should not have lettering on them. Always wear appropriate underwear, it makes a difference.

Blouses – can dress up a pair of slacks, skirt or a suit. Blouses are also suitable in an office atmosphere that has dress down Fridays, where jeans are not permitted however, the dress code is a bit relaxed than Monday – Thursday. Blouses should not be sheer, tight, or ill fitting. For sheer blouses, always wear a camisole underneath or a blazer over the blouse. Always wear appropriate underwear, it makes a difference.

Skirts – may be more colorful, as they match or contrast the blazer/jacket. You may choose a variety of prints as well as fabrics. Be certain to have at least two solid business colors. Seams should never pull and splits should never be in the form of an upside down "V" or the letter "A" as that is an indication that your skirt is too tight/small. Always wear appropriate underwear, it makes a difference.

Pants – similar to that of the skirt. Keeping in mind that you should have some solid colors. For the winter, wool lined pants and for the spring and summer time, linen and cotton blends. Pants should not be ill-fitting. If your underwear lines and your shape are evident, the pants are inappropriate for the work place. Also, make sure the pants are an appropriate length. Always wear appropriate underwear, it makes a difference.

Dresses – remember conservative. Even if the job has an after work function, keep it conservative because you are still in a work atmosphere. Also, you do not want to be the latest negative water cooler gossip, the following morning. You also want to be taken seriously when it is time to get a promotion. Dresses, as with all of your attire, should not be tight, revealing, sheer, etc. Always wear appropriate underwear, it makes a difference.

Overall seasons, colors, and fabrics

Spring/Summer – light, cool colors, pastels, flower prints, linen, cotton, silk, light denim, polyester blends, rayon.

Autumn - earth tones such as orange, brown, leafy greens, leathers, suede, cotton and polyester blends & denim.

Winter – dark, warm colors, navy blue, chocolate brown, black, wool, leather, denim, and cotton and cotton blends.

My personal color charts

Complete the charts below: be specific as possible when making my notes

Because of my _____ skin
tone, my most flattering colors are:
> brown
> black
> navy
> pink
> orange
> green
> yellow
> or
> _____

Because of my _____ hair
color, my most flattering colors are:
> blue
> brown
> black
> navy
> pink
> orange
> green
> yellow
> or
> _____

Notes about colors and me

_____
_____
_____
_____
_____
_____

A list of the colors that I use most and why

_____
_____
_____
_____
_____
_____

List the colors that I want to use but have not. Why?

_____
_____
_____
_____
_____
_____

My Sizes

These are basic things that you should know as a young lady. Please keep in mind that some things are subject to change as you age. Also, be aware of the fact that your shoe size may vary from your boot size. Additionally, depending upon the designer cut will depend on your size, as well.

Clothes

My pant size is:
My dress size is:
My suit size is:
My blouse size is:
My skirt size is:

Underwear

My panty size is:
My brassiere (bra) size is:
My slip size is:
My camisole size is:
My pantyhose size is:
My sock size is:

Footwear

My shoe size is:
My boot size is:
My sneaker size is:

Outerwear

My hat size is:
My coat/jacket size is:
My glove size is:

A Young Lady and Finances
By Tiffany "The Budgetnista" Aliche

Work brings profit, but mere talk leads to poverty.
~Proverbs 14:23

The bible teaches that "the *love* of money is the root of all kinds of evil" (1 Timothy 6:10), not money itself. This distinction is very important. Money is not bad or good, it is a tool that you can *choose* to use for bad or good. For example: A hammer is a tool, and it can be used to build a house or to destroy one. The hammer itself does not decide, the person wielding it does. It is the same with money. Ask yourself; How will I decide to use money? Will I use it to help or hinder others? Will I be generous? Will I live in lack or abundance?

Give freely and become more wealthy; be stingy and lose everything. The generous will prosper; those who refresh others will themselves be refreshed. ~Proverbs 11:24-25

While thinking about these questions I do not want you to confuse money with wealth. According to the dictionary, wealth isthe abundance of valuable resources or material possessions, or the control of such assets. Wealth is not just about money. It is about resources, fullness, having an overflow. It is my hope that you live a whole-fully wealthy life; this includes spiritual, mental, physical as well as monetary wealth. In order for you to do so, there are three lessons that you should commit to memory. These lessons are: you reap what you sow, giving is receiving and blessings equal abundance.

You Reap What You Sow

48

To sow means to plant and to reap means to pick. As a young woman it is essential that you master this life lesson; whatever you plant, you will one day pick. We see this even in nature. For example, apple trees grow from apple seeds, and orange trees grow from orange seeds. You will never see apple trees growing from orange seeds, because what is sown is what is reaped.

The interesting part of this lesson is that when you sow good things, God often lets you reap MORE than what you sow! Is that great news? Just look at how a tiny seed can grow into a giant tree. This means God rewards good things with great things. Why do you think that is? Has that ever happened to you? I'm sure it has. There are many examples in your life where you have reaped (more than) what you've sown. Writing important things down is a key component when trying to learn a lesson, so I have provided a chart for you. In it I want you to write down 10 things you have sown and what you have reaped as a result. Choose 10 positive things, and let this be a constant reminder that you bring wealth into your life by want you plant.

Honor the LORD with your wealth, with the first fruits of all your crops; then your barns will be filled to overflowing, and your vats will brim over with new wine.
~Proverbs 3:9-10

What I have sown	What I have reaped
1)	
2)	
3)	
4)	
5)	
6)	
7)	
8)	
9)	
10)	

Giving Is Receiving

How can giving be receiving? As we discussed in the previous section, what you plant is what you pick. Giving is a form of planting. When you give your time, money, energy and resources to help others, you are really giving to yourself. God teaches us that to give to others, is to give to Him, and we know how generous God can be. When you give to Him, He can give back even more! The important thing to remember is, to **give without expecting anything in return**.

Each of you should give whatever you have decided. You shouldn't be sorry that you gave or feel forced to give, since God loves a cheerful giver (2 Corinthians 9:7). This means you should give from your heart and give because you want to, not because you want something in return. The seeds of true wealth are planted in this way.

It is important that you give on purpose. I have provided a chart where you can write down how you can give to others. Fill it out now, and then plan when you will turn the words you've written into action.

Ways That I Can Give To Others
1)
2)
3)
4)
5)
6)
7)
8)
9)
10)

Blessings Equal Abundance

The dictionary states that a blessing is a special favor, mercy, or benefit. A blessing is any good thing received. We are constantly blessed each year, month, week, day, hour, minute, and second, because life itself is a blessing. God blesses you for two different reasons; for you to enjoy and benefit from, and for you to share that blessing with others. Blessings are never yours alone to keep. They are given to be given. You are blessed to be a blessing. When you revive, it is a signal that you have abundance. What does that mean? Abundance means, extremely plentiful, wealth, overflow. So when God blesses you, He is letting you know that you have *more* than enough. He's letting you know it's ok to give to others because you have extra. BLESSINGS = ABUNDANCE.

Take time now to think of all the ways you are blessed. How have you enjoyed these blessings? How have they made your life better? Have you shared your blessings with other people? How? Use the following chart to help you find ways to identify your blessing, ways you can enjoy them, and ways you can share them with others.

My Blessings	How I Can Enjoy Them	How I Can Share Them With Others
1)		
2)		
3)		
4)		
5)		
6)		
7)		
8)		
9)		
10)		

Wealth is not a gift given only to someone older, or of a specific race or a select group of people. Wealth can be yours the moment you allow yourself to receive it. God is *always* giving. The question is; are you allowing yourself to receive? Remember the lessons and the words you have written. They will help to draw and maintain true wealth for you.

Final Wealth Lessons

Write these down on index cards and put them in a place where you can see them daily. They are your Wealth Reminders

1) Spend less than you make, invest and save the rest.
2) Happiness comes from within.
3) Live out of abundance not lack.
4) Claim what you want and always say you have.
5) Generosity breeds wealth.
6) You often receive *more* than what you give.
7) Blessings are meant to be enjoyed and shared
8) Focus on what *is*, not what isn't.
9) Favor is not always fair. Sometimes you may have to wait for your good things. Patience is not about waiting, it is about how you behave during the wait.
10) Chase your dreams, not money.

I leave you with this. There are three traits that yield success to anyone that possesses ALL of them in abundance.

Crystallized Focus: knowing exactly what you want

Extreme Hustle: willingness to work harder and longer than everyone else
Positive Attitude: maintaining joy even when things don't seem joyful
Do you possess these characteristics? If not, you can. Begin working on them now, because when you harness these three things, wealth is sure to follow.

Chapter Five

A Day in the Life . . . .

"Come, follow me," Jesus Said, "and I will send you out to fish for people." ~Mark 17

Darlene Aiken

Left to right from top to bottom: *Susan L. Taylor, former Editor-In-Chief, Essence Magazine, Ilyasah Shabazz, daughter of Malcolm X, Iman Shumpert, NBA Player, Tashera Simmons, DMX's ex-wife, me at the Wendy Williams 500th Episode party, Edith Washington, Great great granddaughter of Dr. Booker T. Washington, with mentees, with cheerleaders and models during a Macy's sponsored event, being recognized by the WNBA at Madison Square Garden, and the some graduates of one of my eight-week programs, along with members of Sigma Gamma Rho Sorority, Inc., and Latonya Blige, & Taniella Jo Harrison.*

Chapter Six

Cyber Bullying

*"Hold firmly to My teaching and never let go. It will mean life for you.
Don't follow the bad example of cruel and evil people. Turn aside and
keep going. Stay away from them."*
~Proverbs 4:13-15

Cyber Bullying

Before delving into any topic, as an educator, I like to first begin defining the core subject matter, in an attempt to place all involved on the same accord. According to the Webster's dictionary, a **bully** is *"a rough browbeating person; esp: one habitually cruel to others who are weaker. The earliest meaning of English bully was 'sweetheart'. Later bully was used for anyone who seemed a good fellow, then for a blustering daredevil. Today, a bully is usually one whose claims to strength and courage are based on the intimidation of those who are weaker."* Add modern-day technology to the aforementioned definition and now we have the term, "cyber bullying".

It is not a surprise, by now, that there is a growing concern about the lack of social skills that today's youth possess, as a result of technology. I have personally witnessed teenagers sitting next to each other texting one another. Their reasons for this vary from privacy issues, to not having the courage to really express themselves, to just simply enjoying the experience of texting or speed texting. While young people see themselves as "enjoying" the experience, parents and educators are concerned that they are addicted to cyber space and all that comes with their "cyber life".

The reasons as to why cyberspace is so appealing to so many vary. For children who are still in the developmental stages of their self-esteem, this medium permits them to be the person that they really dream of, without immediate retaliation. For example, when two people are interacting face-to-face, there is a chance for one to interrupt the other. In addition to finding out that their words or actions may not be truthful via self-expression. When engaging in cyberspace, one is able to create, or build, if you will, the kind of person that she wishes to be, without interference.

Couple the above with a lack of supervision and this makes a great recipe for bullying via cyberspace also known as cyberbullying. Cyberbullying as with bullying, in general, stems from a low or lack of self-esteem, as stated earlier. However, I want to state something that too many people have not. Yes, teachers, principals, and other school officials play an integral part in the monitoring of this type of behavior, but I would like to see more parents held accountable for the actions of their children's, self-esteem and behavior. Lack of supervision is only the tip of the iceberg.

In today's society, there are far too many parents who want to be friends with their children. Adults who seek to befriend children are in need of serious psychological assistance. Children need and want parents to operate within their roles, whether they know it or not. Children need a safe haven to run to for refuge and parents who provide love, food, clothing, shelter, and discipline can be trusted. Different people have their various takes on corporal punishment vs time out, this is not what I am talking about, right now. However, what I do know is that children need to be challenged and confronted. They need to have adults who will let them know, firmly, when they are out of line, need to re-think decisions, work harder in school, help them define what friendship means, as well as help them love themselves. The key to this is knowing that in some instances, love means having to say, "no!" That two-lettered word must be said, even if that means their daughter cries. That two-lettered word must carry consequences if it is not obeyed, and it is imperative that parents follow through with those consequences.

I am always interested in looking at a subject matter in its entirety. Therefore, based on the aforementioned definition, the person who is the bully is perceived to be strong and the person being bullied is weaker. I don't beg, but I do differ. I also maintain that the person who is the bully is weaker and wishes to strip the person that she is bullying from something. She also is hiding a weakness about herself, and is acting from a basis of fear.

Dr. Nikki Crick, Director of the Institute of Child Development and Distinguished McKnight University Professor, speaks about relational aggression and its effects, cannot be ignored. In other words, boys are physically aggressive and more prone to fight. Girls are more prone to become aggressive via their relationships, which oftentimes is played out in gossip and spiteful acts, such as isolating their victim. Sociologists also have a term that is referred to as the triad group (a group of three) which can also lead to isolation. The thing with the triad group that makes it stand out is that the person who becomes isolated is not usually the last person that dissembled the dyad (a group of two) by joining but rather an older member joining forces with the newest member thus creating an atmosphere of jealousy.

Relational aggression is extremely dangerous because it oftentimes goes unaddressed. One of the primary reasons it is not addressed is because it is intangible. Another reason is, simply, adults do not know how or care to address it as it is just brushed off as lacking importance because it's "what kids do!" that is a huge mistake. It's a mistake on several levels, but the first is that it assists with the building of barriers.

Once barriers are set, girls may not feel a sense of protection and feel as if they must take matters into their own hands or may feel deserving of ill treatment by others. For those that might tell their parents, particularly their mothers, the response is usually the all familiar, "don't worry about it", chalking it up to jealousy.

For girls with a healthy self-esteem, their handling of these types of situations will be different, and their mother's responses will be, as well. Please keep in mind that these are usually not a series of one-sided events. Oftentimes, girls initiate types of behavior that they are not prepared to receive. When this occurs, they may find themselves in a situation that they felt good about inflicting but find great difficulty bouncing back from. This is why I am not a proponent of slang and nicknames.

We must begin to look at the situation well before it gets to the cyber bullying stage. What type of relationship does the bully have with her parents/guardians? Do her parents know what to look for? Parents must be more proactive about getting to know their children past the point of physical features. Behavior changes when major, or what they perceive to be major, things in their lives change, much like adults.

I speak from personal experience, in that, while as a child, I was not privy to computers, but I was a bully. As the older sibling, I always felt it was my duty to protect. This was especially true in areas that I viewed as being unfair (refer to the child development chart that I've supplied in Appendix I). This feeling of wanting to protect did not only apply to my little brother, but related to my friends and my parents, as well. I became upset with my mother when she would discipline my brother. Although she did not have to discipline him much as he was the more meek and compliant child, but when she did, I did not like it.

During my years as a child, being the overweight tall girl with the ponytails who sat in the front of the class in the first row because I was "cursed" with having a last name that began with the letter A, I was, I felt, forced to fight or be the victim of bullies, both girls and boys. Being called names, being taller than my third grade teacher as well as the rest of the students was not something I looked forward to facing every day.

While I had parents who loved me and nurtured me, they were not privy to *all* of the daily school mishaps. The teacher telling the others to, "calm down" or "stop" were not enough. As the target, I decided that I could either remain the victim of "snaps", "ranking", and such peer abuse or I could become an abuser and have people laugh at my jokes that I would make about others. I also decided to take my height and weight and use it to my advantage. So, I began turning the tables and became the bully. Being the bully worked for me because now, people feared me. I like that they feared me because they listened to me, even if I was wrong, but more importantly, they did not mess with me. The name calling, at least to my face, stopped. In addition, I set the stage and was the director of the show. My clothes were not a joke to people, my ponytails were fine, and I now possessed an authority that I didn't have before and it felt great!

Words hurt! Negative words that we place value on hurt even more when, in our minds, they are confirmed by those who are deemed to be prettier, smarter, more popular, etc. Words are damaging to the psyche and children can be cruel. One of the biggest lies told is that "......but words will never hurt me!" Well, words may not physically break our bones, but they can break our spirits, if we are not careful.

Adults are not always equipped to appropriately handle the situation, regardless of their level of education and expertise. Adults, many times, are dealing with their own self-esteem issues.

So, am I proponent of being a bully? Most definitely not! What I am suggesting is that we begin to channel children's energy in a manner that negative energy is turned into something positive. In school, administrators and teachers might begin implementing a cooperaative kind of learning so that students help each other on every subject and they switch groups for each subject. What happens, now, is that each student has an opportunity to teach and each has an opportunity to learn, but all will have an opportunity to become a leader. In addition, each student becomes committed to her own learning to carry out her leadership qualities, but also learns as a leader that she is responsible for others. When we are responsible for others, we are invested in their success.

For parents, yes, in today's society, parents must work. In some instances, they must work several jobs just to make ends meet. However, it is essential that we make quality time for our children. I am a strong advocate of eating together. I find that we take eating very seriously. We do not want to eat with just anyone. Think about lunch time. At lunch, we anxiously seek out certain people to eat with. That same eagerness needs to be applied to our families.

As a child my father worked two jobs during the week and was off on weekends. My mother worked but had two days off during the weekday but had to work on the weekends. On Saturday morning, my brother and I looked forward to morning breakfast. My father would whip up great southern breakfasts, which were a real treat. What we did not know was, he was getting into our heads and hearts, without us feeling interrogated. In fact, we volunteered information at that breakfast table each Saturday morning. My father knew things about neighborhood and school friends that some of their own parents did not know.

What I also came to realize was, I no longer began to feel like I needed that false sense of power. My bullying ceased. I found that I had more friends and these were genuine relationships that continue to this day. What does that have to do with cyberbullying?

In an age where everything is computerized and is electronic, too many parents have not caught up. When parents are removed from situations, their children know. Children are too immature to handle things in the manner of an adult, even if they're the smartest one in their classes. Even if life throws them a curve ball and they are forced to grow up more quickly than their peers. However, children are smart enough to know how to fool parents into believing that just because they are getting good grades in school, they are not victimizing others. This prompts the parental response, "not my child!"

Dr. Teresa Taylor Williams is a practicing mental health professional and owner and publisher of "New York Trend Newspaper". She states, *"The first line of defense for any issues involving your children and their peers is communication. Parents need to be proactive in having a serious discussion about becoming an accomplice to acts of cyber bullying without recognizing their involvement. Parents need to enforce rules of computer usage and monitor their children's associations with friends and question them about the nature of their discussions. For children, they need to be educated by parents and teachers and responsible adults to be aware of friends they might think are victims of bullying. Most importantly, children need to learn the difference between teasing, kidding and the more serious intimidation tactics of a bully. Finally, innocent children need to be able to go to an adult they feel confident will be able to successfully address the issue and not fear becoming a victim of the bully for reporting an incident to an adult.*

The frightening factor about kids who are bullies is that they can become adults who abuse. Every child with a computer can easily become a victim of this deadly form of resentment and hate. Don't' retreat into the comfort of saying, 'not my child'. The parents of Phoebe Prince* may have thought the same."

The example that I often use is the following: parents are supposed to be the eagle on the mountaintop and children are the pigeons in the valley *(please indulge the varied genus for the purpose of illustration)*. When the eagle that is wiser sees trouble headed toward her brood, she sweeps down and saves her little ones from danger. The little pigeons are upset because they are having fun with their friends and do not understand why mom/dad is interrupting such a great game, but come to learn why later as they, too, see the trouble pass from the safety of their protected nest. The other eagle who saw the same trouble nearing but decided to let her brood continue playing so that her little ones would not be upset with her, later on realizes, when it's too late, that she should have helped her little ones as now they were hurt so badly that their wings were clipped and they may never fly at all again. Now, this mother is upset with herself as well as her children are upset with her and will constantly blame their mother for not helping them escape trouble, even when she saw it coming and could have prevented it. In both instances, we are aware that pigeons always remain in the vicinity because they're unable to soar in the manner of an eagle much like many children. Therefore, it is the responsibility of the parent to act on behalf of the child(ren). One of the key things to remember during the parenting process is that, parents should strive to not raise perpetual children, rather independent adults.

When there isn't anyone for children to answer to, but "friends" parents are reduced and a lack of respect sets in. surely, when children lack respect for their own parents, it becomes that more difficult for other adults to gain respect i.e., teachers. In such cases, character building does not take place in the appropriate manner as the elementary subject of respect must first be addressed because it was not addressed in the home. When character building has not taken place in the appropriate stages then you have children whose self-esteem becomes idle. As a result, these children become angry because they're not afforded the same opportunities as their counterparts who have parents that provide boundaries. Confront children in their wrongdoing, as well as hold them accountable for their actions and provide consequences based on their actions or lack thereof.

This is the case for girls because they naturally have serious issues with self-esteem whether they have parents that hold them accountable or not. When parents do not fulfill their roles then children are forced to become the parent in many instances which is additional pressure.

*Prince was a 15-year –old Irish teenager who immigrated to New Have, Mass and came to national attention following her Jan. 14 2010 suicide. An investigation launched by the district attorney discovered that Prince had been a victim of extensive bullying and harassment by her peers and that most o f the adults involved were aware of the teen's torture but chose not to intervene. *(Google)*

Chapter Seven

A Young Lady & Her Body

"The lifestyle of good people is like sunlight at dawn that keeps getting brighter until broad daylight. The lifestyle of the wicked is like total darkness, and they will never know what makes them stumble."
~**Proverbs 4:18, 19**

A Young Lady & Her Body

The Women's Encyclopedia of Health and Emotional Healing By Denise Foley, Eileen Nechas, and the Editors for Prevention Magazine Health Books (1993)

AIDS – One million women are affected. The cause-Human immunodeficiency Virus (HIV). It is transmitted by the exchange of body fluids through genital contact. Some symptoms may be: none for years, ARC (AIDS Related Complex) eventually develops with such symptoms as persistent swollen glands and chronic infections that don't respond to medication. Malignancies or severe infections develop when the immune system is compromised. **Diagnostic tests:** blood test determines presence of HIV antibodies. **Treatment:** Experimental drugs.

Chlamydia – Four million women are affected per year – 1.3 to every woman. The cause is Chlamydia trachomatis bacteria. It is transmitted by direct contact with infect mucous membranes and secretions in genitals, mouth and throat. 75% of women have no symptoms. For those that do, the signs appear 1-3 weeks after exposure, they include: burning urinations, unusual vaginal discharge, abdominal pain, painful intercourse and bleeding between periods. The tests consist of taking a sample of vaginal secretions. **Treatment:** Antibiotics. **Complications:** pelvic inflammatory disease. Infants exposed during birth may develop eye infections or pneumonia.

Genital Herpes – 30 million affected about 500,000 each year (2 women to each man). Caused by Herpes Simplex Virus. Transmitted by direct contact with an active sore or virus-containing genital secretions. Can lie dormant for

70

months or years. Can be transmitted even when there are no symptoms. **Symptoms** – generally develop 2-20 days after exposure. Blisters or bumps appear which may itch, burn or tingle. May cause flu like symptoms with first outbreak. May cause painful urination. Recurrences are likely. Tests are conducted by taking a sample from a sore. **Treatment:** see your doctor. **Complications:** self-infections of eyes, fingers and other body parts possible if infected area is touched. Babies can be infected during birth.

Genital Warts – 1 million each year. The cause – Human Papilloma Virus (HPV). Transmitted by direct skin-to-skin contact with an infected person during sex, whether warts are visible or not. **Symptoms** – warts appear in or near vagina several weeks to 9 months after exposure. May appear raised or flat, singly or in multiples. Often no symptoms and usually painless, but can cause itching and burning. Tests – direct visual examination, and pap smear. **Treatment:** your doctor may apply a liquid to gradually remove the warts. Warts may be removed by freezing or burning. Surgery is occasionally needed to remove large warts. **Complications:** strongly associated with cervical cancer.

Syphilis – 130,000 each year (1.3 men to every woman). Caused by Treponema pallidum bacteria. Syphilis is transmitted by direct contact with ulcers of someone with active infection. The germs can also pass through broken skin on other parts of the body. Untreated infected people (even with mild or no symptoms) can infect others during first two stages of the disease – up to 2 years. **Symptoms:** painless, open sore, called a chancre, appears in or near vagina within 10 days to 3 months after exposure. Later symptoms include skin rash over body or on palms of hands and soles of feet and flu like symptoms. All may vanish, but the infection may not, unless treated. Tests include: blood tests and microscopic identification bacteria using a sample. **Treatment:** antibiotics. **Complications:** bacteria can damage heart, eyes, brain, spinal cord, bones and joints. Can cause miscarriage or birth defects. Babies acquire the infection in the womb and may develop symptoms later in childhood.

Trichomoniasis – 3 million each year. The cause – trichomoniasis vaginalis protozoan. Transmitted – through intercourse. **Symptoms** – heavy, yellow green or gray vaginal discharge, abdominal pain, discomfort during intercourse and painful urination occur within 4-20 days after exposure. Tests – microscopic examination of vaginal fluids. **Treatment:** see doctor. **Complications** – bladder or urethra inflammation.

Ladies, keep in mind that since the book where this information was derived, many of the treatments and number of infected people have changed. If you are experiencing any of the above symptoms or have reason to believe that you have been infected, please speak with your parents/legal guardians about having you checked out, immediately by a licensed professional. Please keep in mind that oral sex is sex and you can contract an STD via oral sex. Abstinence is the only 100% way to be STD free.

Chapter Eight

Herbs, Vitamins, Minerals, Grains, and Spas, Oh! My!

"Carefully guard your thoughts because they are the source of true life. Never tell lies or be deceitful in what you say. Keep looking straight ahead, without turning aside. Know where you are headed and you will stay on solid ground."
~Proverbs 4:23, 25, & 26

Herbs, Vitamins, Minerals, Grains, and Spas, Oh! My!

Earlier, we spoke about setting the table, now we are going to touch upon the topic of foods. Foods that nourish your body and keep you looking and feeling great. Remember the famous cliché, "You are what you eat". I have found this to be more than a cliché. When I eat foods that do not have nutritional value, I become prone to a variety of allergies, colds, I begin to feel lethargic, irritable, and my skin tells on me. The irritability will especially kick in right before "Aunt Flo" makes her monthly visit. However, when I eat live foods and foods packed with vitamins, minerals, and nutrients, I am lively, irritable free and "Aunt Flo" isn't such a nuisance, in fact, she's quite pleasant.

I have provided you with a list of some things that I have eliminated from my eating regimen or eat sparingly. This was a process and did not occur overnight. Honestly, I was somewhat rebellious, initially because I did not know of healthy replacements. Once I began to become more educated about what my body required to function properly I just did what I had to. Now, I eat better and feel better than I have ever felt. Also, I believe that eating healthy will keep you looking younger longer.

Before eliminating foods, I strongly suggest that you and your parents make an appointment with a professionally licensed health care practitioner. Everyone's body is different, so make sure you are aware of what your body needs or may not require. An expert can advise you on how and when to eliminate foods according to your individual need.

All right, brace yourself! All pork products *(please note that pork is hidden under different names in things such as cakes, breads, pies, juices, and cookies)*. Packaged meats and cheeses can be extremely high in sodium. White food products, for example, flour, sugar, rice, prepared cereals, frosted cereals (too much white sugar and possibly hidden animal byproducts), canned and frozen foods, coffee, tea (except certain herbal), cookies, cakes, pies, ice cream, dairy, anything with preservatives (the reason behind by transformation). Sulphite and its derivatives are used as a preservative to retain color is wine, dried fruits, and salads. Watch out for signs on salad bars that list sulphites to retain the color of fruits and vegetables, as this preservative has been known to cause asphyxia – blockage of the throat, which could lead to death.

You may be thinking, at this point – what can I eat? Before I answer that, I want to share something with you that may be somewhat disappointing, but change is usually not an easy feat, but worthwhile. Your parents may be thinking, when they enter into the health food store to shop for the alternatives, that the transformation is expensive. However, I challenge you to shift your paradigm (your way of thinking). Begin to subscribe to the notion that you pay now or pay later. The problem with paying later is that you pay with your health. So, pay with your money, now, and preserve your health. After all, money is not meant to hold onto, but health is.

Below, is a partial listing of hidden animal ingredients in foods that we eat on a regular basis. **Source: *The Complete Idiot's Guide to Being a Vegetarian by Suzanne Havala, Ms. R.D., F.A.D.A., Food Lover's Companion by Sharon Tyler Herbst, The Vegan Sourcebook by Joanne Stephaiak, M.S. Ed.***

Hidden animal ingredients.

Albumin – the protein component of egg whites. Albumin is also found in animal blood, milk, plants, and seeds. To thicken or add texture to processed foods.

Anchovies – small, silvery fish of herring family. Worcestershire sauce, Caesar salad dressing, pizza topping, Greek salads,

Animal shortening – butter, suet, lard, packaged cookies and crackers, refried beans, flour tortillas, ready-made pie crusts.

Carmine (carmine, cochineal, or carminic acid) – red coloring made from ground-up insects. Bottled juices, colored pasta, some candies, frozen pops, "natural" cosmetics. We get caught up into thinking because it says, "natural" that it's good for us.

Calcium stearate mineral – typically derived from cows or hogs, garlic salt, vanilla, meat tenderizers, salad dressing mixes, caric acid (decanoic acid), animal fats added to ice cream, candy, baked goods, chewing gum, liquor and often not specified on ingredients lists.

Casein (caseinate) - A milk protein. It coagulates with the addition of rennin and is the foundation of cheese. An additive in dairy products such as cheese, cream cheese, cottage cheese, and sour cream. Also used in adhesives, paints, and plastics.

Clarifying agent - Derived from any number of animal sources. Used to filter wine, vinegar, beer, fruit juice, soft drinks.

Gelatin - protein from bones, cartilage, tendons, and skin of animals, much of the commercial gelatin is a by-product of pig skin - marshmallows, yogurt, frosted cereals, gelatin-containing desserts, molded salads.

Glucose (dextrose) - fruits or animal tissues and fluids. Baked goods, soft drinks, candies, frosting.

Glycerides (mono-, di-, and triglycerides - Glycerol from animal fats or plants. Processed foods, cosmetics, perfumes, lotions, inks, glues, automobile antifreeze. Used as an emulsifier.

Isinglass - gelatin from air bladder of sturgeon and other freshwater fish. Clarify alcoholic beverages and in some jellied desserts. Rarely used now.

Lactic acid. - Acid formed by bacteria acting on the mile sugar lactose. Imparts a tart flavor. Cheese, yogurt, pickles, olives, sauerkraut, candy, frozen desserts, chewing gum, fruit preserves, dyeing and textile printing.

Lactose - saccharum lactin, D-lactose, milk sugar. Culture medium for souring milk and in processed fods such as baby formulas, candies and other sweets, medicinal diuretics, and laxatives.

Lactylic stearate - Salt of stearic acid. Dough conditioner.

Lanolin - waxy fat from sheep's wool. Chewing gum, ointments, cosmetics, waterproof coatings.

Lard - rendered and clarified pork fat. Often fat from abdomens of pigs or the fat around the animal's kidneys. Baked goods.

Lecithin - Phospholipids form animal tissues, plants, lentils, and egg yolks used to preserve, emulsify, and moisturize food. Cereal, candy, chocolate, baked goods, margarine, vegetable oil sprays, cosmetics, and ink.

Lutein – deep yellow coloring from marigolds or egg yolks. Commercial food coloring.

Myristic acid (tetradecanoic acid) - Animal fats, chocolate, ice cream, candy, jelled desserts, baked goods.

Natural flavorings - Unspecified, could be from meat or other animal products, processed and packaged foods.

Oleic acid (oleinic acid) animal tallow (see tallow below) - Synthetic butter, cheese, vegetable fats and oils, spice flavoring for baked goods, candy, ice cream, beverages, condiments, soaps, cosmetics.

Palmatic acid animal or vegetable fats - Baked goods, butter and cheese flavoring.

Pancreatin (pancreatic extract) - cows or hogs digestive aids.

Pepsin – enzyme from pigs' stomachs with rennet to make cheese.

Propolis – resinous cement collected by bees. Food supplement and ingredient in "natural" toothpaste.

Rennin (rennet) – a coagulating enzyme found in a young animal's stomach. Rennin is used to curdle milk in foods such as cheese and junket – a soft pudding like dessert.

Royal jelly – substance produced by glands of bees. "natural foods" and nutrient supplements.

Sodium Stearoyl Lactylate – may be derived from cows, hogs, animal milk, or vegetable mineral sources. Used in cake, pudding, or pancake mixes, baked goods, margarine.

Stearic acid (octadecenoic acid) – tallow , other animal fat and oils. Vanilla flavoring, chewing gum, baked goods, beverages, candy, soaps, ointments, candy, soaps, ointments, candles, cosmetics, suppositories, and pill coatings.

Suet – hard white fat around kidneys and loins of animals. Margarine, mincemeat, pastries, bird feed, and tallow.

Tallow solid – fat of sheep and cattle separated from the membranous tissues. Waxed paper, margarine, soaps, crayons, candles, rubber, and cosmetics.

Vitamin A (A1, retinol) vitamin obtained from vegetables, egg yolks, or fish liver oil, vitamin supplements, fortification of foods, "natural cosmetics".

Vitamin B12 - vitamin produced by microorganisms and found in all animal products; synthetic form (cyanocobalamin or cobalamin on labels) is vegan supplements or fortified foods.

Vitamin D (D1, D2, D3) - D1 is produced by humans upon exposure to sunlight, D2 (ergocalciferol) is made from plants or yeast, D3 (cholecalciferol comes from fish liver oils or lanolin supplements or fortified foods.)

Whey – watery liquid that separates from the solids (curds) of milks in cheese-making. Crackers, breads, cakes, processed foods in cheese-making..

My Herbal Cupboard

The herbs below are usually in my cupboard either in root, leaves, flower, powder, and oils

Red Clover – immune booster, blood purifier, and other values.

Sea Moss – rich in vitamins and minerals, except iron.

Echinacea – best when used at the onset of a cold, immune booster.

Goldenseal – expels phlegm and mucus.

Eucalyptus – antiseptic, great for breaking up phlegm lodged in the chest and good when used in aromatherapy.

Dandelion – body toner, loaded with minerals.

Chickweed – known for breaking down cellulite, rich in vitamins and minerals.

Cayenne – stimulates the circulatory system, burns toxins off the stomach, nerve tonic and it's good to put a little in your socks in the winter to keep feet warm. (do not take on an empty stomach).

Rosemary – good for seasoning, headaches, and hair tonic.

Sage – antibiotic, seasoning food, carminative.

Chamomile – good for overcoming anxiety, anger and tension.

Boneset – excellent for expelling mucus and phlegm.

Bladderwrack – excellent for expelling mucus, stimulant, thyroid tonic and more.

Lily of the Valley – good brain strengthener.

Pau'D Arco – immune booster, fights off viruses and a host of other ailments.

Astragulus – immune booster, increases and maintains energy.

Dong Quai – good for female concerns.

Mother Wort – good as a heart tonic, uterine stimulant.

Hawthorne Berries – excellent for heart flutters.

Nettle – rich in vitamins and minerals, good for anemia and allergies.

Mullein – sedative, excellent for the alleviation of allergies and aids in sleeping.

Cascara Sagrada – a gentle but powerful laxative.

Hops – great for inducing sleep and eases headaches.

Lavender – great for relaxation and fragrance.

Shiitake Mushrooms – good for digestion, cholesterol in the liver, immune booster.

Horsetail – excellent for strengthening fingernails and hair.

Myrrh – antiseptic and good for disinfecting your tongue and strengthening your gums.

Red Raspberry – rich in minerals, immune booster, great for female concerns.

Definition of Terms

Astringent – provides a protective coating and is soothing to the mucus membranes.

Diuretic – assists with the flow of your urine.

Sedatives – calming enough to induce sleep

My friends, colleagues, and family are always teasing me about my herbs. Some refer to me as "Mother Earth". Whenever someone calls me and asks what I'm doing? If I tell them that I am eating, they laugh and ask if I'm eating leaves again. I'm accustomed to the mockery and know that it is a term of endearment. Additionally, these are the same people who call upon me when they have questions about what to take for certain ailments.

Teas

I rarely if ever drink soda. However, commercial juices have far too much sugar and ingredients that I can live without. I prefer herbal tea – hot or cold. I enjoy the medicinal properties while being refreshed.

Barks & Roots

Check the packaging until you become an expert and can determine for yourself. Pour fresh filtered water into a stainless steel or glass saucepan (aluminum is toxic!). Add the bark and /or roots to the water. Cover the pot. Boil on a low flame until the essence of the herbs have blended with the water. Boil longer for a stronger tea, less for a lighter tea. Steep for 30 minutes, strain and drink. If you must sweeten the tea, (which I do not recommend) use grade A Maple Syrup or raw (not heated) honey.

Leaves & Flowers

Pour fresh filtered water into a stainless steel or glass saucepan. Bring the water to a boil over a low flame. Once the water begins to boil, turn the flame off and place the leaves into the water and cover. Let stand for approximately 30 minutes. Longer for stronger tea. Strain and drink. See above for sweetening tea.

Capsules

I have become skeptical of capsules whenever I am not in the area of my special health food stores. However, I rely heavily on my herbs, so I buy them in bulk as well as capsules. Because I am a vegetarian (the only flesh I eat is fish). Many times, gel caps contain ingredients that I no longer ingest, see the list above. Therefore, I purchase vegetarian formula capsules. I crush and/or mix my herbs and put them into capsules. I base the herbs that I put into each capsule on my current need. Not only am I getting great capsule, but I can address whatever my symptoms are and know what is in each one. This is also an excellent way to transport herbs, whenever I am traveling. All I have to do is request hot water or bottled water and I am good to go. However, I only recommend this for those who have a great knowledge of herbs.

Fruits & Vegetables & Grains

The fruits and vegetables I try to keep in my home are not only because they are full of vitamins and nutrients, but it's a great way to replace harmful snacks, if you are a big "snacker", as I can be. Especially during that time of month, we begin to crave foods that may not necessarily be good for us. Train yourself to eat properly now, so that eventually, it will be a way of life for you and not a diet.

Here's my Inventory:
Fruits

I try to not purchase seedless fruit. Every living thing began in seed for, including humans, therefore, if the fruit does not have a seed, where did it come from?

Oranges, grapes, apples, pears, lemons, bananas*, water cocoanuts*, mangoes (my absolute favorite), pineapples*, plums, berries, avocado, melons, peaches, pomegranates, ginoppes, limes, papaya, raisins, tomatoes, kiwi, and figs.

* Fruits are matured, ripened ovaries of flowers. There are three basic types of fruits: single, aggregate and multiple. The pineapple is an example of a multiple fruit. About 100 or more flowers are crowned together and after fertilization, the young fruits begin to swell. There is not enough room for each to develop separately and so they become fused. The pineapple is also an example of a parthenocarpic plant which produces fruits without fertilization of the ovules. Seeds are usually absent but sometimes about 10 to 15 tiny seeds (3to5mm long and 1 to 2 mm wide) can be found in an average size pineapple. There are many types of bananas. Some have seeds and some without seeds. In commercially cultivated bananas, the banana fruit forms without pollination of the flower. Its development is fully parthenocarpic. The pulp develops mainly from the ovary wall of the flower. Wild bananas have seeded fruits that develop only if pollinated.

Coconut is monocotyledon. The fruit wall of the coconut can be divided into three layers epicarp, mesocarp and endocarp. The epicarp is smooth and hard which changes color from green to yellowish brown when ripe. The fibrous husk is the mesocarp and the endocarp is the stony layer surrounding the endosperm, which is the seed. The meat of the coconut is the solid endosperm and the juice is the liquid endosperm. **A Guide to Fruits and Seeds by Anne Nathan & Wong Yit Chee Singapore Science Center (1987)**

Vegetables

Spinach, collard greens, dandelion leaves, string beans, arugula, cucumbers, new potatoes, watercress, sprouts, romaine lettuce, green and red leaf lettuce (avoid the popular and inexpensive iceberg lettuce as it does not have any nutritional value), Swiss chard, radicchio, celery, okra, kale, mustard greens, pumpkin and all kinds of squash (my son used to call squash "squish" when he was little).

Grains

Whole & rolled oats, quinoa, cous cous, barley, basmati rice, wild rice, bran, millet, buckwheat, amaranth, bulgur, grits, kamut, kasha, millet, seven grain cereal, and textured soy-protein concentrate.

Store your grains in airtight containers away from light, moisture, and heat.

Trust me, this took years of experimentation and studying to develop this habit and I'm still evolving and encourage you to do likewise. As a result, this way of life involves shopping quite often. Reason being, you want your fruits, vegetables and grains to be as fresh as possible. I am accustomed to picking fruits and vegetables from an organic garden (except the root or earth vegetables that have worms and bugs attached – I'm squeamish when it comes to bugs).

Flour

Most of us are accustom to white flour, however, white flour has no nutritional value via the processing that it endures, which includes the bleaching process. To add more of a nutritional and flavorful kick, try healthier flours such as, amaranth, bran, buckwheat, cornmeal (yellow or blue), oat, rye, spelt, wheat germ, and whole wheat, research which is

86

best for you and check the gluten content of each if you have allergies.

Store your flours in a cool, dry, and dark place. I keep mine in the refrigerator, some people suggest placing it in the freezer, I only recommend this if it's a particular flour that you do not use often.

Dried Beans

Baby lima beans, black eyed peas, kidney beans, Garbanzos (chickpeas), cannellini beans, red kidney beans, navy beans, red beans, and great northern beans.

Nuts

Brazil nuts, walnuts, almonds, cashews (which are really seeds from a fruit), macadamia nuts, peanuts, pecans, pistachios, and hazelnuts.

Seeds

Flaxseeds (I prefer the oil), sesame, and sunflower.

Vitamins & Minerals
Let us look into the world of vitamins and minerals. Some herbalists do not believe in vitamins in the form of pills and some do. I happen to believe that we need the vitamins and minerals, however, they should be as pure as you can get them. Let's face it, no one eats properly every single day of her life, therefore, our bodies are being depleted of the vitamins and minerals that we do need.

Below is a general outline of some important vitamins and what it is said to do.

Vitamins

A – promotes healthy skin (helps alleviate acne), hair, bones, vision, teeth and gums.

B1 – good for the nervous system, growth, positive mental attitude and aids in digestion.

B2 – tissue repair, healthy skin, helps the body use oxygen, and vision.

B3 – proper circulation, and healthy skin, aids in the functioning of the nervous system.

B12 – builds rich blood (this is good for those who are anemic) folic acid, and helps balance memory.

C – helps the body fight off infections, reduces stress, good for the skin, gums, may   reduce cholesterol, and more.

D – builds strong bones, teeth, promotes growth in youngsters, good for the nervous system, heart, and blood stream. You can get this vitamin from the sun and green leafy vegetables.

E – promotes healthy blood circulation protects against pollution, good for reproductive organs, tissue repair, useful in treating PMS, fibrocystic disease, and muscles.

Folic Acid – consider a brain food, good for energy, strengthens immunity, body cell growth and healing.

Minerals

Calcium – good for healthy teeth, bones and promotes growth, the maintenance of a regular heartbeat, lowers cholesterol levels, and more.

Iron – aids in growth, prevents fatigue, great for fighting diseases, aids in a healthy immune system

Magnesium – calms nerves, also good for healthy teeth, assists calcium and potassium, can help prevent dizziness, PMS, and more.

Manganese – important to our reproductive systems, good for the nervous system and muscles, fat metabolism (I personally like that!), immunity and more.

Potassium – sends oxygen to the brain, good for clear thinking, heart muscles – bananas and natural sea moss are loaded with it.

Sodium – helps to transport liquids and nutrients from cell to cell, muscle function, blood ph, however, too much can cause problems.

Sulfur – disinfects the blood, helps resist bacteria, great for hair, skin, and nails – MSM and yellow mustard are excellent sources of this mineral.

Zinc – aids in the healing of skin (acne), ph balance, good for the heart and reproductive organs, and more. *Information from the Prescriptions for Nutritional Healing 2nd Edition A Practical A-Z Reference to drug-free remedies using vitamins, minerals, herbs, and food supplements by James F. Balch, M.D. & Phyllis A. Balch, C.N.C.*

Oils

In addition to eating, I use oils for many other reasons, as well. I always use cold pressed extra virgin, whenever possible. Below are some of the oils that I use and how I use them:

Olive – use for cooking, my hair as a hot oil treatment, oil pulling and as a light body oil.

Sesame Seed – use for cooking, mix with other natural oils as a body oil, my hair as a hot oil treatment, and oil pulling.

Coconut – use for cooking, my hair, lips, face, body, seasons my cast iron skillet, and oil pulling.

Grape Seed – salad dressing as it's good for your heart.

Maintenance is Key

If you are still not convinced that you are what you eat, let this marinate in your mind for a moment. When you are sick, your body is craving certain minerals and vitamins take a look at what might be a concern of yours:

Your fingernails – white spots and brittle – got 'em? You may be lacking zinc. Eat more nuts, legumes, green leafy veggies, fish, lima beans, pecans, seafood, and soy beans. Use some horsetail, cayenne, chamomile, dandelion, and nettle tea. Also, I rub fresh lemons on my nail beds after I squeeze the juice into the dishwater, daily to strengthen them.

Your hair – is it dry and itchy? I suggest beta carotene, zinc and eat more nuts and dried fruits (not the ones with the preservative sulphur dioxide). Make some rosemary and sage tea and use as a rinse on your hair.

Your skin – are you experiencing dull, dry and itchy skin (sounds almost like your hair) – drink plenty of filtered water (preferably room temperature), eat plenty of green leafy vegetables and drink sea moss. Chamomile, red clover and goldenseal (do not take for more than a week at a time) herbal teas (without sweetener). Rub some pure Shea butter, olive oil, or castor oil onto your skin after bathing and wear pajamas and socks and lie down for a while.

Your teeth – do your gums bleed or feel week? Try brushing with sea salt (refrain if you suffer from hypertension) and myrrh at least twice per day. Drink plenty of distilled or filtered water. Eat plenty of green leafy vegetables and fruits. Load up on vitamin C. Once per week mix one part hydrogen peroxide with two parts water and rinse your mouth (do not swallow, rinse well). This not only disinfects your mouth, it can help whiten your teeth. Peroxide also cleans your ears, belly button, and your house. Also, to assist with many ailments, including deodorizing your mouth, I recommend oil pulling. Oil pulling is when you place a tablespoon of oil, preferably coconut, into your mouth and swish it around for approximately 15 minutes. Do not swallow. Do not spit into your sink, only spit into the toilet and flush immediately. Once you complete pulling the oil, rinse your mouth thoroughly and then brush your teeth. You should always soak your toothbrush in a covered jar filled with fresh peroxide to kill bacteria. I do not recommend oil pulling for youngsters unless they are being supervised.

Your breath – does your breath have an odor? Try scraping your tongue with a tongue scraper. See peroxide rinse above. Also, take chlorophyll caps or liquid as this is a natural body deodorizer. Try oil pulling. Visit your oral hygienist to make certain everything else is okay.

Your underarms – sometimes take a break from the harsh chemicals that deodorant has. When you change your diet and incorporate more green leafy veggies and live foods, along with adding chlorophyll to your diet, after a shower rub some alcohol onto your armpits and let this take the place of deodorant. Please do not do this right after shaving your armpits. You might also want to try mixing equal parts of pure coconut oil, baking soda, and arrowroot powder and rubbing the paste under your armpits as a natural deodorant. Add a drop of peppermint or lavender oil for scent.

At Home Spa Rejuvenation

For relaxation, I strongly suggest lavender. Relax in some bath salts (check with a licensed health care professional to make sure this is safe for you to do), that you can make yourself. Here is what you will need:

Lavender oil, peppermint tea, tea tree oil, or any essential oils that you prefer (check your local health food store for many of these ingredients) Epsom salt (please refrain from using Epsom salt if you suffer from high blood pressure) vegetable glycerin.

Combine one of the oils with the other ingredients, run your water and scoop out a handful, place it under the running water and get in and relax.

Another way to relax is to make a relaxation pillow. Here is what you will need for your pillow (this was a summer camp favorite while I was growing up): 2 pieces of white organic cotton fabric approx. 14 inches long and 8 inches wide (or whatever size you prefer)

200 cotton balls
1 small piece of lace
1 stick pin
1 small Ziploc bag
1 teaspoon of lavender oil
½ teaspoon of lavender castile liquid soap
1 spool of white polyester sewing thread
1 pair of safety scissors
1 cup of pure lavender leaves

92

1 cup of chamomile leaves (make sure you are not allergic to ragweed and if you are consider a cup of mullein tea, unsweetened, of course)
1 cup of rubbing alcohol
A hot iron (use with supervision)

Wash your organic fabric with lavender castile soap and let it dry. Once it is dry, iron the wrinkles out of the organic fabric. Take your cotton fabric and sew the two pieces together, leaving one end open. Sew by hand and make your stitches as tight as possible to secure your pillow. Iron the inside flaps down. Gently turn the pillow case inside out. Now, mix the herbs, 200 cotton balls, oil and alcohol and place half of the prepared cotton balls into the small Ziploc bag. Gently poke holes into the small Ziploc bag and stuff into the pillow. Take the remaining cotton balls and place into the pillowcase surrounding the Ziploc bag. Sew the small piece of lace in with the stitches, but do not sew it for permanency as this will allow you to replenish the contents when necessary.

Place this on top of our pillows, make up your bed and when bed time comes you will have a fresh scent on your bed. You might want to enhance it with some lavender linen spray, but remember not to overdo it.

Need a Quick Facial?

Take a large bowl, with supervision, (make sure the bowl can withstand heat at boiling temperatures and that the bowl is placed on a firm foundation such as a kitchen table

Add heated water (not boiling)
Add 2 drops of tea tree oil

Place a shower cap over your hair and a towel over your head and let the towel cover the bowl as well

Allow a small opening so that the tea tree will not overpower you and you may breathe

Allow the steam to open your pores for about 5 minutes

Wash your face with your regular facial product

Rinse your face with warm water, then splash your face with cold water to close the pores and give you a refreshing feeling

Add moisturizer and relax.

Facial Exercise

Everyone is always talking about exercise. What about facial exercise?

1.   Every morning and during the day, try the following facial exercises: say your vowels – A, E, I, O, U – but exaggerate each letter – do ten sets.

2.   During the day, while sitting down, put the back of your hand under your chin and hold for a minute or two – do ten sets.

3.   Close your eyes, smile as wide as you can while keeping your lips together – 10 sets.

4.   Fill your mouth with air, switch the air from left to right, repeat ten times.

I have found these facial exercises have kept me from getting a double chin and laugh lines. Much cheaper and safer than botox and cosmetic surgery.

Chapter Nine

My Inner
Beauty Pledge

"Dear friends, don't be afraid of those who want to kill your body; they cannot do anymore to you after that."
~Luke 12:4

The My Inner Beauty Pledge ™ was designed with you in mind. There are going to be times when you do not feel your best, and that is normal. This pledge is something that you will commit to saying on a regular basis, especially during those times when you're feeling a little down. Once you have it committed to memory, you can use it at your leisure. I have also included in the appendix, a pledge that you can frame to hang on your wall. You will be amazed at how words can change your attitude. Now that you have these positive life changing words that you can call your own, I challenge you to go out feeling on top of the world every single day! All you have to do is insert your name in the space below and begin your new journey. Watch how your self-esteem will boost. All of your family and friendswill notice an immediate difference.

My Inner Beauty Pledge ™

I, _____, do solemnly pledge to commit myself to always treat myself with love and respect, at all times. I will always believe that I am smart enough, good enough, and pretty enough to accomplish my goals, dreams and aspirations. I am not threatened by the talents, gifts, and abilities of others. In fact I welcome the talents, gifts, and abilities of others and seek to surround myself with those who are reaching for the stars.

My vision of where and who I want to be is the greatest asset that I possess.

Chapter Ten

My Journal

"And the Lord answered me: Write the vision; make it plain on tablets, so he may run who reads it. For still the vision awaits its appointed time it hastens to the end-it will not lie."
~Habakkuk 2:2-3

My Journal

My Journal

My Journal

My Journal

My Journal

My Journal

My Journal

My Journal

My Journal

My Journal

My Journal

My Journal

My Journal

My Journal

My Journal

My Journal

My Journal

My Journal

My Journal

My Journal

My Journal

My Journal

My Journal

My Journal

My Journal

My Journal

My Journal

My Journal

My Journal

My Journal

My Journal

My Journal

My Journal

My Journal

My Journal

My Journal

Appendix I

Child Development Guide
(not an exhaustive list)

Eight Years Old
Developmental Tasks
- Acquiring a sense of accomplishment centered on achieving greater physical strength and self-control
- Increasing own ability to learn and apply skills, deal with peers, and engage in competition
- Developing and testing personal values and beliefs that will guide present and future behaviors

Indicators Related to Developmental Lag
- Social isolation and lack of friends
- Inappropriate relationships with "older" people (teenagers)
- Stealing, pathological lying, and/or fire-setting

Normal Characteristics
- Drives self until exhausted
- Appetite decreases
- May forget and/or be easily distracted
- Enjoys/wants and withdraw from adults; has strong emotional responses to teacher and may complain that teacher is unfair or mean

Nine Years Old
Developmental Tasks
- Acquiring a sense of accomplishment
- Centered on achieving greater physical strength and self-control

- Increasing own ability to learn and apply skills, deal with peers, and engage income petition
- Developing and testing personal values and beliefs that will guide present and future behaviors

Indicators related to developmental lag
- Excessive concerns about competition and performance (especially in school)
- Extreme rebellion
- Over dependence on caregivers for age-appropriate tasks (combing hair, tying shoes, etc.)

Normal Characteristics
- Busy and active; has frequent accidents
- May be excessive in self-criticism, tends to dramatize everything, and is very sensitive
- Enjoys school, doesn't like to be absent, and tends to talk more about things that happen there
- Wants to know the reasons for things

10 Years Old
Developmental Tasks
- Acquiring a sense of accomplishment based upon the achievement of greater physical strength and self-control
- Increasing the ability to learn and apply skills, deal with peers, and engage in competition
- Developing and testing personal values and beliefs that will guide present and future behaviors

Indicators of related to developmental Lag
- Excessive concerns about competition and performance

- Social isolation and lack of friends and involvements, few interests
- Procrastination (unconcern with competition of tasks

Normal Characteristics
- Differences in physical maturation rates develop (girls before boys)
- Is becoming very independent, dependable, and trustworthy
- Is most interested in friends and social activities
- Individual differences become more marked
- Is very conscious of fairness, is highly competitive, and argues over fairness

11 Years Old
Developmental Tasks
- Acquiring a sense of accomplishment based upon the achievement of greater physical strength and self-control
- Increasing own ability to learn and apply skills, deal with peers, and engage in competition
- Developing and testing personal values and beliefs that will guide present and future behaviors

Indicators Related to Developmental Lag
- Physical symptoms (headaches, nervous stomach, ulcers, nervous tics, bedwetting, etc.)
- Procrastination (unconcern with task completion)
- Social isolation and lack of friends and involvements; few interests

Normal Characteristics
- May have rapid weight increase
- Likes privacy

- Is highly selective in friendships and may have one "best" friend; finds it important to be in the "in" crowd; may develop hero worship
- Is alert, poised; argues logically; is frequently concerned with fads
- Is more concerned with what is wrong that what is right

12 – 15 Years Old
Developmental Tasks
- Acquiring a sense of accomplishment based upon the achievement of greater physical strength and self-control
- Increasing own ability to learn and apply skills, deal with peers, and engage in competition
- Developing and testing personal values and beliefs that will guide present and future behaviors
- Creating personal identity based upon the integration of values
- Developing a sense of self in relations to society, other individuals, the opposite sex, the future, personal vocation, ideas, and the world

Indicators Related to Developmental Lag
- Inappropriate relationships with "older" people
- Stealing, pathological lying, and/or fire-setting
- Extreme rebellion
- Depression, sense of isolation, loneliness
- Suicide attempts; psychosis
- Poor hygiene
- Alcohol/drug abuse

Normal Characteristics
- May have increased possibility of acting on sexual desires (it is imperative that parents are really able to effectively communicate with their daughter)
- May be concerned about appearance of acne
- May become interested in earning money
  Experiences sudden and rapid increases in height, weight, and strength with the onset of adolescence
- Has strong urge to conform to peer-group morals
- Commonly sulks, may direct verbal anger at authority figure
- Withdraws from parents (who are invariably called "old-fashioned")
- Thrives on arguments and discussions
- May read a great deal
- Knows right and wrong; tries to weigh alternatives and arrive at decisions alone

Fifteen to Nineteen Years of Age
Developmental Tasks
- Creating a personal identity based upon the integration of values
- Developing a sense of self in relations to society, other individuals, the opposite sex, the future, personal vocation, ideas, and the world

Indicators Related to developmental Lag
- Delays in physical development
- Impulsiveness, extreme rebellion, pathological lying
- Hatred of family, truancy, running away

Normal Characteristics
- Has essentially completed physical maturation; physical features are mostly shaped and defined
- Worries about failure

- Sometimes feels that parents are "too interested"
- Becomes seriously concerned about the future; begins to integrate knowledge leading to decisions about future

About the Author

Darlene Aiken, nominated in 2013 for the John C. Maxwell Leadership Award, is an internationally bestselling author, respected award-winning leadership authority, self-esteem and personal growth expert, adjunct lecturer, consultant, professional speaker, publisher, and community servant who has dedicated a great portion of her life to teaching transformational principles to girls, tweens, teens, and young ladies. She holds a Masters Degree from Stony Brook University, takes independent study courses at Yale University, and holds a Baccalaureate of Arts Degree from C. W. Post College of Long Island University. She has taught Juvenile Justice, Sociology, Freshman Seminar, and Personal Growth Courses at four and two-year colleges.

Ms. Aiken is also the author of an anthology which is on Amazon's bestsellers list in the Women and Business categories. ***Network to Increase Your Net Worth*** hit the number two spot, the same day of its launch at the end of September 2013.

Ms. Aiken collaborated with other professional businesswomen from across the world for the completion of this bestseller. This book, How to be a Young Lady: Your Total Guide for Being the Best Possible You! is the second edition, which is also published by her new publishing imprint, Inner Beauty Solutions Publishing.

Ms. Aiken's work has been seen in Essence Magazine, News 12, heard on KISS FM – NY & ATL, she has been recognized by the WNBA & NY Liberty, the Hon. Kasim Reed, Mayor of Atlanta, Sigma Gamma Rho Sorority, Inc. with the Beacon of Light Award, a Proclamation from a former County Executive, a popular business newspaper recognized her twice as one on the 50 Top Most Influential Women in Business, her undergraduate alma mater recognized her with the Dean's Alumnus Award, she has received letters of appreciation and recognition from two New York Senators Schumer and Parker, as well as a myriad of additional accolades.

She has held key positions in renowned organizations such as the Rotary Club, NAACP, Urban League, as well as sat on boards for Suffolk County Community College, C.W. Post College of Long Island University, and others. In her positions, she has assisted or in some capacity became involved in the preservation the homes as historical landmarks for great contributors to society such as John Coltrane and Dr. Booker T. Washington. She is currently working with Ilyasah Shabazz and others to do the same for Dr. Betty Shabazz's home in Mount Vernon, NY.

Ms. Aiken is the founder of the award-winning self-esteem, personal growth, and anti-bullying company, Inner Beauty Solutions, Inc., the founder of the national pageant for young women of African descent, the Miss Black Collegiate USA Scholarship Pageant™, and the founder of the, "Exposing Minds, Not Bodies!"™ Empowerment Conference for all Girls. She is the proud mother of a scholar-athlete, who attends college on a full scholarship, as well as is the proud member of the Christian Cultural Center under the tutelage of her pastors, Dr. A.R. Bernard, Sr., Elder Karen Bernard & Elder William Pointer.

To learn about products and services, please call 631.533.4006 or email Ms. Aiken at professordeedee@icloud.com. Follow Professor Dee Dee on @professordee and on @professordeedee

Made in the USA
Lexington, KY
13 June 2014